SS-LEIBSTANDARTE

SS-LEIBSTANDARTE

THE HISTORY OF THE FIRST SS DIVISION 1933–45

Rupert Butler

MBI Publishing Company

This edition first published in 2001 by
MBI Publishing Company
Galtier Plaza, Suite 200
380 Jackson Street
St. Paul, MN 55101 USA
www.motorbooks.com

MBI Publishing Company books are also available at discounts in bulk quantity
for industrial or sales-promotional use. For details write to Special Sales Manager
at Motorbooks International Wholesalers & Distributors, Galtier Plaza, Suite 200
380 Jackson Street, St. Paul, MN 55101 USA.

Library of Congress Cataloging-in-Publication Data available.

ISBN: 0-7603-1147-1

Editorial and design by
Amber Books Ltd
Bradley's Close
74-77 White Lion Street
London N1 9PF

Project Editor: Charles Catton
Editor: Siobhan O'Connor
Design: Peggy Sadler
Picture Research: Lisa Wren

Printed and bound in Italy by: Eurolitho S.p.A., Cesano Boscone (MI)

The author would like to thank Charles Messenger for allowing him to draw generously on his book,
Hitler's Gladiator (Brassey's, 2001), the biography of Sepp Dietrich. Thanks are also due to James Lucas,
author of *Hitler's Elite: Leibstandarte 1933–45* (Macdonald & Jane's, 1975), who patiently answered a
number of queries and provided additional details about the division and the *Waffen-SS*.

Contents

CHAPTER ONE

FOUNDATION

After her defeat in World War I, Germany was ripe for revolution, with various gangs fighting for power on the streets. Cocooned by bodyguards and followers addicted to ongoing violence, Adolf Hitler sought protection in the creation of a new elite, the *Leibstandarte Adolf Hitler*.

Newsreel propaganda films produced in Nazi Germany during the life of the Third Reich featured footage of elite members of Heinrich Himmler's *Schutzstaffel* (SS Protection Squad), immaculate in their black and silver uniforms, standing like robots before the Berlin Reich Chancellery. These were the troops of the *Leibstandarte SS Adolf Hitler*, responsible for the safety of their Führer, a bodyguard contingent destined to rise under the clash of arms to become the premier panzer division of the *Waffen-SS*.

Those who served in the *Leibstandarte* and in the armed SS as a whole enjoyed a special status and glamour, the remnants of which, even amid the ashes of defeat, the dwindling number of veterans are keen to preserve. There is some justification for this. The armed echelons of the *Schutzstaffel*, with their double-S runic sleeve flash and belt buckles inscribed with the motto *Meine Ehre heisst Treue* ('My Honour Is Loyalty') fought with considerable bravery on the front line during World War II. What this does not take into account, however, and what apologists to this day conveniently

Left: Contingents of the *Leibstandarte* assemble as their Führer's Guard of Honour during the Nuremberg Rally of 1937, notable for Hitler's assurance that the Third Reich would last for 1000 years.

ignore, are the many crimes of brutality which can be laid directly at the door of the *Leibstandarte*.

ORIGINS

To reach the truth means taking a look beyond the popular image of the immaculate uniforms and marching bands of these SS paragons. The origins lie deep in a Germany still in the shadow of the 11th day of the 11th month of the year 1918. Kaiser Wilhelm II, who had vainly intended to abdicate only as German Emperor, but still retain his rights as King of Prussia, had finally taken his withered arm and shattered imperial ambitions into exile. For the army, rich in the traditions of battle triumphs stretching back to the days of Frederick the Great, there was a legacy of shame and submission at its enforced emasculation by the victors, following the Treaty of Versailles. But for many whose husbands, brothers and sons had perished on the battlefields of France and Flanders, there was weary resignation and a longing to be rid of militarism. There was little sympathy for those that found the Allied terms unacceptable and even less for the notion that, in the words of Philipp Scheidemann, first Chancellor of the Weimar Republic, the 'hand should wither' before any shameful demands – 'intolerable for any nation' – were agreed by signature.

Other voices of resentment and fury, however, drowned all calls for moderation. Mass meetings were held throughout the country which were ripe with sullen threat to national order. Aggression soon followed. Cities became minor battlefields – convenient areas of violence for a variety of terrorist groups such as the Spartacists, forerunner of the German Communist Party, and groups of ex-servicemen formed as the *Stahlhelm* and the *Freikorps*, who clashed with the manpower of the *Reichswehr*, the standing army acting as the Chancellor's Guard. In Bavaria, a Soviet-style regime assumed power with an optimistic programme of land reform, workers' control and participation in government. Although such heresies were defeated with consummate savagery, the legacy of Bavarian socialism was to be the birth of a new

Above: Members of the *Freikorps* dismount from lorries in post-war Berlin. The *Freikorps* was a right-wing organisation staffed by former soldiers, and a number were later to join Hitler's *Sturmabteilung*, or SA.

movement. Adolf Hitler, its chief architect, was fuelled by two hatreds: the teachings of Karl Marx and, above all, a loathing of Jews, whom he saw as 'rats, parasites and bloodsuckers'.

During World War I, Hitler had served as a Lance Corporal (*Gefreiter*) in the 16th Bavarian Infantry (List Regiment). Before his discharge, he had attended one of the soldiers' indoctrination classes with which the *Reichswehr* supplemented its armed combat of left-wing subversion. As a *Bildungsoffizier* (Instruction Officer), he received orders to investigate – in fact, spy on – a collection of nationalist veterans and beer-swilling nationalists, as well as general misfits, who made up the all but bankrupt *Deutsche Arbeiterpartei* (German Workers' Party). The group certainly had some resonance for Hitler, especially where the fifth of its 25 Points was concerned: 'None but members of the nation may be citizens of the state. None but those of German blood, whatever their creed, may be members of the nation. No Jew, therefore, may be a member of the nation.'

The future Führer joined as Party Member No. 555 and, by January 1920, had emerged as its leader. During the next month, in an impassioned speech held in a Munich beer hall, he demanded the adoption of all 25 points. He was already thinking ahead, however, and planning a far more radical programme, paramount to which was the demand that all Jews be denied office and citizenship. The name of the party was changed that April to *National-sozialistische Deutsche Arbeiterpartei* (the NSDAP, or National Socialist Party).

FOUNDATION

Before long came the call for a campaign of hate and subversion where blood would literally spill onto the streets of German towns and cities. In such dangerous times, none was exempt from the threat of violence, party leaders and would-be dictators least of all. Hence, in 1923, came the emergence of the *Stabswache* (Headquarters Guard), a pretentious name for the activities of its two leading strongmen, Joseph Berchtold, a stationer, and Julius Schreck, a chauffeur, both of whom were assigned a crude bodyguard role by Hitler. This pair were joined by several adherents who were, for the most part, labourers from the lower middle or working classes of Munich, the likes of Ulrich Graf, butcher by trade and amateur boxer by night; Emil Maurice, a watchmaker with a criminal record; and Christian Weber, a penniless former groom.

The *Stosstrupp* (Shock Troop) *Adolf Hitler*, which incorporated the *Stabswache*, at first consisted of some 30 thugs much addicted to punch-ups with opponents and the copious use of boots, knives, blackjacks and rubber truncheons. These toughs, many of them recruited from the *Freikorps*, in time became members of the infinitely more powerful *Sturmabteilung* (SA, or Storm Troopers). This was the creation of *Freikorps* leader Ernst Röhm, who built up a 2000-strong private army, boosted by *Freikorps* volunteers who became SA storm troopers. The original *Stabswache*, nevertheless, does deserve at least a footnote in the history of pre-war Germany, laying as it did the foundations for a force responsible solely to Hitler with the task of protecting him from all enemies, by whatever method and, if necessary, with individuals' lives. The *Leibstandarte* of the future was to exist essentially for the same purpose.

On 9 November 1923, a crucial event took place, although few foresaw its repercussions at the time. In Munich, a 600-strong group of SA, led by Hitler, made an ill-judged bid to snatch power from the nationalist and rigidly independent leaders of Bavaria and proclaim a new government, in the so-called Beer Hall Putsch. This intended political coup was an embarrassing failure which degenerated into semi-farce, at a cost of around a dozen *Stosstrupp* lives, SA casualties and short-term imprisonment for Hitler. While Hitler languished in Landsberg jail, the various factions became even more fragmented and uncontrollable. On release, Hitler made up his mind. He had need for a single, cohesive protection force.

In April 1925, eight men came together to create a new *Stabswache*. Within two weeks, it had become the SS, destined to be controlled by the myopic *Reichsführer-SS* Heinrich Himmler, the one-time industrial chemist who was dedicated to the pursuit of homeopathy, herbal cures and, most of all, dreams of a racially pure Germany. Even within the tight embrace of the SS, however, Hitler wanted the services of men who would be loyal to him exclusively, as he made clear in one of his countless dissertations:

'Being convinced that there are always circumstances in which elite troops are called for, I created in 1922–23 "the Adolf Hitler Shock Troops". They were made up of men who were

Left: The Munich Putsch, 9 November 1923. The bespectacled figure with the Imperial Eagle flag is Heinrich Himmler, future *Reichsfuhrer-SS* and supreme chief of the Gestapo and the *Waffen-SS*, including the *Leibstandarte*.

ready for revolution and knew that some things would come to hard knocks. When I came out of Landsberg everything was broken up and scattered in sometimes rival bands. I told myself then that I needed a bodyguard, even a very restricted one, but made up of men who would be enlisted without conditions, even to march against their own brothers, only 20 men to a city (on condition that one counts on them absolutely) rather than a dubious mass ... But it was with Himmler that the SS became an extraordinary body of men, devoted to an ideal, loyal to death.'

DIETRICH THE BAVARIAN

Hitler had no intention of being saddled with a 'dubious mass'. Less than two months after coming to power as Chancellor of the Reich in January 1933, he turned to an old party comrade and former bodyguard, Josef (familiarly known as 'Sepp') Dietrich, a strong-jawed, thick-accented Bavarian, and former artilleryman. That same year, in May, Dietrich was able to report to Hitler that he had formed a headquarters guard of loyal SS men titled the *SS-Stabswache Berlin*, conveniently quartered near the Reich Chancellery. Then came two more *Stabswache* incarnations, with two more successive changes of title. First, there was the *SS-Sonderkommando Zossen* (Special Commando), a designation which signified something of the guard's elite character. Secondly, as a result of its merger with *Sonderkommando Juterbog*, it received first the title *Adolf-Hitler-Standarte*. Then, at the behest of Hitler himself, this was changed to *Leibstandarte SS Adolf Hitler*, (SS Bodyguard Regiment Adolf Hitler), a name chosen deliberately to prompt memories of the old Bavarian Life Guards.

The announcement of the name change was made on the last day of the Nazi Party rally held in the Luitpoldhalle at Nuremberg in September 1933, nine months after Hitler came to power. The ceremonial event, staged with all the elaborate spectacle that Propaganda Minister Joseph Goebbels could muster, carried the self-confident title 'Congress of Victory'. Here, the towers of Kleig lights shone on 60,000 Hitler Youth, parading with the slogans of 'Blood and Honour' and 'Germany Awake'. At the rear of the stage was the German eagle, its talons enclosing the golden laurel-wreathed swastika, and beneath which stood 60 stalwarts of the SS in their uniforms of black and silver, their dress swords drawn and shouldered.

Once Hitler had arrived precisely at 1700 hours, flanked by *Reichsführer-SS* Heinrich Himmler and Reinhard Heydrich, head of the Reich Central Security Office, he took his place on his podium. The spectators were then treated to a lengthy, bombastic speech lasting over an hour, the overall theme of which was 'the reward of virtue' (*Turgenheld*). Deserving of such rewards, Hitler made clear, were

those who had kept the faith, not only with him personally, but also to the ideals of Germany and National Socialism. Keeping that faith had meant conducting a ceaseless, ruthless campaign against treachery, wherever it was manifest. Special tribute was paid to Heinrich Himmler – 'my Ignatius Loyola' – and to those who served with him, Hitler's faithful guards, his *Stabswache*. It was to be their reward to have a special name created for them, 'a name indelibly associated with that of their Führer'.

A sardonic presence at Nuremberg that day was a correspondent from the *New York Times* newspaper, who found Hitler's revelation 'singularly uninteresting after all the guff that had preceded it ... All we got for our pains was the knowledge that henceforth his *Stabswache* would be officially known as *Leibstandarte*

Below: Hitler in Berlin in May 1927, surrounded by early adherents of the fledgling Nazi movement. He is followed by Julius Schreck (in peaked cap), one of his original bodyguards, who also acted as Hitler's chauffeur.

Right: Hitler acknowledges the crowd from a window in the Chancellery after the 'Night of the Long Knives' in 1934. Below him stand members of his bodyguard, the _Leibstandarte_, who had taken an active role in the purge.

SS Adolf Hitler.' At the time, no one could guess, of course, how significant for Germany that change of name was going to be. One man who showed more than a proprietary interest was, naturally enough, Himmler. And therein lay the seeds of conflict. From the very start, it was obvious that Hitler intended this new organisation to be an elite, responsible and answerable to him. This was underlined graphically by yet another spectacular event.

On 9 November 1933, 11 months after Hitler became Reich Chancellor at the Munich Feldherrnhalle War Memorial in the Odeonplatz, some 830 men were mustered, facing the Theatinerkirche. The streetlights were extinguished and the square lit solely by torches. In a Wagnerian touch, at midnight, after the last strike of the bell from the Theatinerkirche, Hitler arrived, accompanied by Himmler; General Werner von Blomberg, the Minister of Defence; and _Gruppenführer_ Sepp Dietrich, who presented his life guard for swearing in.

SWEARING THE OATH

First came a paraphrase of the SS oath, spoken by Heinrich Himmler: 'We swear to you, Adolf Hitler, loyalty and bravery. We promise this to you and will be obedient until death.' Then, from the SS men came recital of the full oath: 'I swear to you, Adolf Hitler, as Führer and Reich Chancellor, loyalty and bravery. I vow to you, and those you have named to command me, obedience unto death. So help me God.'

To at least one SS observer, Emil Helfferich, it was a moment of ecstasy. Helfferich referred to 'splendid young men, serious of face, exemplary in bearing and turnout. An elite. Tears came to my eyes when, by the light of torches, thousands of voices repeated the oath in chorus. It was like a prayer.' From that year on, newly enrolled members of the _Leibstandarte_ who had yet to take their oath were sent to Munich for the annual ceremony held in front of the Feldherrnhalle.

Himmler remained insatiable for as much power as possible. He constantly pointed out that Hitler's own guard was, from the moment of its inception, firmly wedded to the SS, and was fond of quoting the Party's Organisation Book. 'The original and most important duty of the SS is to serve as the protector of the Führer ... By decree, its sphere of duties has been enlarged to include the internal security of the Reich.' This declaration, Himmler assumed, entitled him to regard the _Leibstandarte_ as his own territory, as, in theory at least, he ultimately commanded it.

The reality was somewhat different. It was Sepp Dietrich who had the direct ear of the Führer and from whom Himmler took his orders. This inevitably led to conflict between Dietrich and Himmler. In the words of an indignant Himmler, the *Leibstandarte* was 'a complete law unto itself. It does and allows anything it likes without taking the slightest notice of orders from above.' Dietrich's opinion of the other man was made abundantly clear to his American interrogators after the war: 'This guy tried to imitate the Führer. His appetite for power could not be satisfied. On top of this he was a great hand at hoarding and scrounging. He received money from everywhere and everybody … I had quite a number of rows with Himmler.'

This was an understatement. Himmler, with his icy stare behind granny spectacles, could reduce many SS subordinates to quaking jelly. By contrast, Dietrich, contemptuous of social niceties and frequently foul-mouthed into the bargain, had no such respect. On one occasion, during the course of a discussion between the two men, Dietrich exploded: 'My position as guard commander will no more allow your interference on security matters than it will upon the morality of my men. They are mine and we are Hitler's. Now go back to your office and let us get back on with the job.'

The responsibilities of the *Leibstandarte* grew. The highest profile remained that 24-hour guard duty outside the Chancellery and, particularly, the Führer's residence in Berlin's Wilhelmstrasse. This last presence especially struck visitors to Nazi Germany in the early years of Hitler's power. Among them was the British MP Henry ('Chips') Channon, who wrote in his diary: 'No one is allowed to walk immediately in front of it, and sentries motion one to cross to the other side of the street.'

It was not long before the black-uniformed SS had taken over inside the Chancellery. Visitors were obliged to pass through three rings of SS guards before it was possible to get anywhere near Hitler. Guests at the Führer's table were served by bright, young waiters in neat, white jackets, *Leibstandarte* men. When Hitler ventured out, he was ensconced within a posse of open, black limousines filled with the SS in their full dress uniforms.

From *Leibstandarte* members had also sprung the *Führerbegleitkommando* (FBK, or Escort Commando), a handpicked detachment of some 40 men, 10 officers and 30 enlisted men. Their role was not only one of routine guard duty, but also to act as orderlies, valets and couriers. They were also required to serve as soldiers at short notice. Although those who were not considered of battle material were ruthlessly weeded out, many *Leibstandarte* men later attested that Hitler had taken a personal, even paternal, interest in their wellbeing. Dismissals were infrequent. Here the Führer exhibited a calculated self-interest; those dismissed from the 'family' were prone to be potential security risks.

THREAT FROM THE SA

Hitler, meanwhile, had other preoccupations, not least of which was the threat posed by Ernst Röhm, who had remained one of the most dedicated of his early followers. As chief of staff of the SA, Röhm had under his control two and a half million storm troopers, together with a seat in the Cabinet. Röhm had his own ambitions, however, and a Cabinet post was not enough to keep him quiet.

The crunch came in February 1934, when the SA leader presented to the Cabinet a proposal to set up an entirely new Ministry of Defence, embracing a People's Army, the SS, the SA and all veteran groups. Such an idea was plainly insupportable, particularly in light of this belligerent statement by Röhm: 'Anyone who thinks that the task of the SA has been accomplished will have to get used to the idea that we are here and that we intend to stay here, come what may.'

Hitler acted. In June 1934, Dietrich secured the transport necessary to lift the *Leibstandarte* to southern Germany, together with a supply of arms. Two companies of the *Leibstandarte* were sent from Berlin to Kaufering, outside Munich. Orders given to Sepp Dietrich were direct and brutal: he was handed the

Above: On 30 January 1937, during celebrations for the fourth anniversary of the Nazi's ascension to power in Germany, Hitler greets *Leibstandarte* commander Sepp Dietrich (in helmet).

names of six prominent SA men and told to organise a squad and go to the Stadelheim prison in Munich, where the prisoners – former friends and colleagues, incidentally — were held and shoot them. Dietrich arrived with 'six good shots to ensure that nothing messy happened'. After some delay, the executions, amateurish and messy, went ahead. Figures as to just how many perished in what ultimately became known as 'The Night of the Long Knives' are confusing, although many sources have quoted 150 victims of the firing squads. Ernst Röhm was among them. Those who survived, in the words of Gerald Reitlinger in his *The SS: Alibi of a Nation*, 'found themselves members of an organisation as innocuous as the Women's Institute movement'.

Apart from Dietrich's role in the blood purge of the SA dissidents, the *Leibstandarte* was also active

elsewhere. Members of mobile squads, designated *Einsatzkommandos* (Action Commandos), were let loose with the remit to snatch anyone with even the remotest connection with dissidents. The addiction of these mobile squads of the *Leibstandarte* to patent gangsterism – which could be compared to the activities of the likes of Al Capone in the United States – is graphically illustrated by the manner of the killing of Erich Klausener, a director in the Transport Ministry and President of the Catholic Action. *SS-Hauptsturmführer* Kurt Gildisch, who described himself as 'an enthusiastic National Socialist', entered

15

Klausener's office building and encountered his victim on the way to the washroom. Gildisch, seemingly in no hurry, escorted Klausener back to his office and told him he was under arrest. Klausener then turned his back on Gildisch, searching in a cupboard for his jacket. The SS killer drew his weapon and fired. In a bid to make the killing look like suicide, Gildisch then placed his Mauser near the body's right hand and, before leaving, put a double guard on the door. His eventual reward was promotion to *Sturmbannführer*.

THE SS FORMATIONS

In the wake of the purge of the SA, all who dared to oppose the regime lived under the shadow of the enhanced power of the SS, the supreme arbiter of terror in Hitler's Germany, which emerged with three militarised formations. These were the *Leibstandarte SS Adolf Hitler*, the *SS-Verfügungstruppe* (SS-VT, or Special Purpose Troops, designated the *Waffen-SS* in 1940) and the *SS-Totenkopfverbände* (Death's Head detachments).

The SS-VT had its origins in the early development of Germany as a police state, where the slightest hint of civic disobedience and unrest was not tolerated. Conveniently, the SS-VT emerged from an organisation already to hand. This was the *SS-Politische Bereitschaften* (Political Readiness Squads), consisting of full-time armed units of company strength. Eventually, the squads were absorbed into the SS-VT, but it was from these squads that the *Leibstandarte* received its early training. In the course of a secret order, dated 2 February 1935, Hitler set out his vision of the SS-VT, which was to consist of three *Standarten* or regiments, together with an engineer and signals battalion. In the event of war, the SS-VT was to be 'incorporated into the Army. They are then subordinated to military law which also apply to matters of recruitment.' The Army also maintained some control over the SS-VT, notably in the fields of military training and the right of inspection.

Hitler felt keenly the need to proclaim to the German people the virtues of National Socialism, the SS-VT and, in particular, the *Leibstandarte*. An

opportunity to do so was afforded by the holding of a plebiscite in the Saarland on 12 January 1935, which resulted in its inhabitants voting overwhelmingly – 477,000 to 48,000 – to return the coal-rich territory to the Reich. Hitler, anxious to visit the Saarland, entrusted some of the escort duties to the *Leibstandarte*, which would provide an excellent showcase for the emerging power of National Socialism. The Army had been slow in coming forwards for the escort role and was put firmly in its place. The Führer proclaimed: 'If the army is reluctant to lead the way, a suitable spearhead will be provided by the *Leibstandarte*.'

At the end of February, around 16,000 men — Dietrich's motorcycle company, two line companies of the 1st Battalion, two companies from the 2nd Battalion and one from the 3rd – arrived in Saarbrücken. The reception accorded the *Leibstandarte* was ecstatic, as reflected in this hyperbole from one newspaper: 'Hitler's men – they are as Gods come to show the way for the new Germany.'

Sepp Dietrich's star was already high. The former baker's boy, farm labourer, waiter and chauffeur who, by the end of World War I, had reached the rank of *Oberfeldwebel* (sergeant major) had, in 1929, been elevated to the rank of *SS-Standartenführer* (colonel) for his work in organising the SS in southern Bavaria. Dietrich rose to *Oberführer* rank less than a year later, taking command of *SS Abschnitt Süd* (SS Section South). From then on, there was a straight career progression from *SS-Gruppenführer* in 1931 to *SS-Obergruppenführer* in July 1934, and ever upwards.

The prestige of the SS-VT – and with it the *Leibstandarte* – ran in parallel with Dietrich's own rapid promotions. By May 1935, membership of the SS-VT was regarded as military service with the armed forces and, in the following year, the SS-VT had acquired its own general staff, with an SS-VT inspectorate commanded by ex-*Reichswehr* Lieutenant

General Paul Hausser. Lest any section of the SS-VT entertain lofty ideas, Hitler was ever present with stern reminders such as the injunction that the SS-VT 'forms no part of the Wehrmacht nor of the police. It is a permanent armed force at my disposal.' Hitler went further. Matters of recruiting and training in ideological and political matters were to be in the care of the *Reichsführer-SS*. He emphasised, however, that Himmler's role would be 'in accordance with directives issued by me'. The message was clear: in Army matters, the Commander in Chief was to be the sole authority.

Conflict between the SS-VT and the Army was inevitable. The Wehrmacht, with no small degree of snobbery, considered the SS-VT to be beyond the pale socially, as well as being political upstarts. There were frequent complaints that members of the SS refused to salute Army officers; there were instances

of unseemly brawls. One man who helped to bridge the gap and formed an immediate rapport with Dietrich was General Heinz Guderian, revered as Germany's leading exponent of armoured warfare and commander of XVI Panzer Corps. Dietrich learned that he would be under Guderian's command for what, in March 1938, Hitler was terming the 'liberation' of his native Austria, his self-proclaimed mission to return that country to Germany.

One incident illustrated the extent to which Dietrich had the ear of the Führer. In his memoirs, *Panzer Leader*, Guderian wrote: 'It seemed to me that the Anschluss [union] should be completed without any fighting. I felt that for both countries it was an occasion for rejoicing. It therefore occurred to me that as a sign of our friendly feelings the tanks might well be beflagged and decked with greenery. I asked Sepp Dietrich to enquire if Hitler would give his approval to this, and half an hour later I was informed that he did.'

Positive Reception

Everywhere, the reception was joyful. World War I veterans with decorations pinned to their chests lined the streets. Flowers and food were pressed on the contingents of the *Leibstandarte* who joined Guderian's panzer units after their long drive from Berlin. Hitler, who had set off for Vienna, received a tumultuous welcome, while the detachment from *Leibstandarte SS Adolf Hitler*, charged with his safety, strove to keep up with their Führer's breakneck progress, flanking his car.

The *Leibstandarte*'s members could be forgiven for reflecting with some satisfaction that it had shown up well in comparison with the Army. The much-vaunted panzer units had experienced mechanical trouble on the road from Salzburg, and had been left stranded. An angry Guderian brushed this aside, defending his troops by saying that the

Left: Nazi contingents, including a detachment of the *Leibstandarte*, pass through the streets of Innsbruck on 4 April 1938. After this *Anchluss* (Union), Hitler said that returning Austria to Germany had been his earthly mission.

Right: A company commander of the *Leibstandarte* gives a radio interview in Wenceslas Square in Prague while civilians listen in. The *Leibstandarte*'s vehicles have been covered with greenery for the occasion.

breakdowns were trivial. Whatever the truth, the men of the *Leibstandarte* had covered no less than 965km (600 miles) in some 48 hours. Cooperation with the Army had been total. The 2nd Panzer Division remained in the area of Vienna until the autumn, when it was replaced by Austrians. The *Leibstandarte* and the staff of XVI Army Corps returned to Berlin in April.

Hitler next turned his attention to Czechoslovakia, issuing on 20 May his directive for Operation Green (*Case Grun*), the occupation of the Sudetenland with its German minority. Once again, the *Leibstandarte* took part in the invasion under the command of Guderian's XVI Panzer Corps and, again, the tanks were draped in greenery. For Hitler's entry, a guard of honour was made up of three companies, one each from 1st Panzer Regiment, 1st Rifle Regiment and the *Leibstandarte*. This incursion was followed six months later by occupation of Bohemia and Moravia.

Wehrmacht Rivalry

Three SS regiments – *Leibstandarte*, *Germania* and *Deutschland* – had taken part in the Czech occupation, a role which did not please the stiff-necked echelons of the *Oberkommando der Wehrmacht* (OKW, or German High Command). A press release was issued from OKW declaring that the occupation had been the work of 'the Army, Air Force and the Police'. This by no means satisfied Hitler, who took a blue pencil to the statement and reworked it as: 'This joyful operation was carried out by units of the Army, the Air Force, the Police and the *Leibstandarte*.'

Particularly noteworthy are the later remarks about the SS which would be made by General Ludwig Beck, who was the last peacetime Chief of the German General Staff: 'It was interesting to observe that an organisation that Hitler had categorically stated would never bear arms in military operations, and was in no sense intended to rival the army, was now taking part in every coup the Führer pulled off.' Beck added to this observation significantly: 'Not only were they taking part, but they were, by 1938, wearing the army uniform instead of their own, except on ceremonial occasions.'

The hint of uneasiness conveyed by Beck's utterances were not lost on the upper echelons of the

Wehrmacht. Hitler could not afford to antagonise the Army High Command and reiterated his undertaking that only the Wehrmacht should bear arms for the Reich. Police operations, it was implied, were really beneath the dignity of the Army, with its long and fine traditions. Such diplomacy was not, however, echoed by Himmler, who declared '... If the army want to hold aloof from such dirty work when it is ordered, it must be prepared to tolerate the special force that exists for such jobs.'

The conflict and rivalry between the Wehrmacht and the *Waffen-SS* was still in its early stages, but it was there nonetheless. Since the Führer's territorial ambitions were by no means slaked, there was patently a need for a strong military force. Hitler's guard was determined that it would be in on the act.

CHAPTER TWO

ORGANISATION

As Hitler's personal bodyguard, the *Leibstandarte* was often in the public eye, and the unit recruited only those who fitted the Nazis' strict racial criteria. Recruits were required to read only approved Nazi tracts, and civilians were encouraged to look up to these 'Aryan supermen'.

Within the recruitment and training methods applied to the men of the *Leibstandarte* there were, of course, practices that were applicable to all military forces preparing for war. But the difference for those of the *Waffen-SS* was that they were often governed by the strict ideological tenets of National Socialism, a condition of service which led to clashes with the Wehrmacht.

The source of such disagreements can ultimately be traced to Heinrich Himmler, to whom the *Leibstandarte* represented personal wish fulfilment. Himmler was described by Walter Dornberger, a veteran of the *Reichswehr*, as 'like an intelligent elementary schoolmaster, certainly not a man of violence'. Indeed, he seemed the very antithesis of anything remotely militaristic; his background was academic and one of solid, middle-class respectability, with a childhood of iron discipline.

It is perhaps scarcely surprising that Himmler was drawn to the Army, even if, by the time he was able to join the 11th Bavarian Infantry Regiment in 1918 at the age of 18, there was no place for him. The

Left: The strict parade-ground training at the *Leibstandarte*'s Lichterfelde barracks led them to be dubbed 'asphalt soldiers' by the Wehrmacht, but they were expected to be immaculately presented at all times.

armistice robbed him of any chance of military service; one year later, he went on to enrol as a student of agriculture at the Technical High School, Munich University. Himmler's preoccupations with his studies were allowed but one deviation: an obsession with his health and physical fitness. His efforts to achieve it were ludicrous – he could not even reach the parallel bars in the university gymnasium. He also assiduously attended the Munich students' duelling and shooting section. When eventually he secured a duel for himself, the result was five cuts from his opponent, for which he received five stitches and a ligature. By all accounts, Himmler was delighted.

RACIAL IDEAS

Alongside the quest for physical fitness, Himmler was absorbing deep-seated racial preoccupations, the dream of Germans as a master race. Thus it is possible to understand the motivation which later led him to insist of his Black Guards that their appearance should be what he assumed to be strictly Nordic. He declared: 'I insist on a height of 1.70 metres. I personally select a hundred or two a year and insist on photographs which reveal if there are any Slav or Mongolian characteristics ...' Every man must be 'of well proportioned build; for instance there must be no disproportion between the lower leg and the thigh, or between the legs and the body; otherwise an exceptional bodily effort is required to carry out such long marches ... The point is that in his attitude to discipline the man should not behave like an underling, that his gait, his hands, everything, should correspond to the ideal which we set ourselves.'

As for standards of physical perfection – which, ironically, would have firmly barred him from membership of his own elite – the *Reichsführer-SS* declared with pride: 'Until 1936, we did not accept a man in the *Leibstandarte* ... if he had even one filled tooth. We were able to assemble the most magnificent manhood into the *Waffen-SS*.'

It was far from being enough. From the end of 1935, every SS man was required to produce a record of his ancestry: for officers, these had to extend back to 1759; for other ranks, 1800. 'Undesirable blood' was therefore rejected; any would-be recruit who was later found to have been mistaken as to his provenance or had deliberately lied was subject to instant expulsion. An SS instruction laid down: 'A decision to join the Führer's military force is equally nothing less than the expression of a voluntary determination to continue the present political struggle on another level.'

MARRIAGE CHECKS

Sepp Dietrich's views on Himmler's racial obsessions are not precisely known, but can perhaps be guessed at. Certainly he had been known to grumble: 'Some 40 good specimens at least are kept from joining the *Leibstandarte* every year due to doubt concerning racial ancestry.' Preoccupation with race extended deep into a *Leibstandarte* man's personal life. If he wished to marry, for instance, his would-be bride had to submit her ancestry for examination, together with a photograph of herself in a bathing costume.

For training, there were Himmler's *Junkerschulen* (SS cadet training centres), but Dietrich had been determined that his *Leibstandarte* should have a setting worthy of them. The great showpiece was Lichterfelde Barracks, the main gate of which, in the mid-1930s, had the appearance of a sullen office block. Between 1940 and 1941, all that had been

transformed. The main gate, entered from a pleasant tree-lined street, was now dominated by two heroic-sized statues of overcoated soldiers who wore coal-scuttle helmets. Topped by an eagle and a swastika, the words '*Leibstandarte Adolf Hitler*' were writ large.

At each corner of an enormous rectangle were large dormitory blocks, designated 'Adolf Hitler', 'Horst Wessel', 'Hermann Göring' and 'Hindenberg.' Within the rectangle were the classrooms and instructional facilities. In the reception area of the barracks were furnishings of the finest oak, the walls inscribed with Nordic runes inlaid in silver, together with their translations. Frescoes lionised the achievements of Germany and, above all, those of Frederick the Great, Hitler's greatest inspiration. Several service buildings included the vast Feldmarschall Saal dining hall which could seat 1000 cadets for a single meal.

A Protestant chapel used by the *Leibstandarte* and also by the people of the Berlin-Lichterfelde area stood in the command building which was situated on the south side. Here at the entrance stood statues of the four Kings of Prussia, Friedrich William I, Friedrich II, Friedrich Wilhelm III and Wilhelm I. Another indication of the *Leibstandarte*'s bid for exclusivity was the use of such terms as *Bataillon*, *Kompanie* and *Zug*, in preference to the Nazi-paramilitary *Sturmbann*, *Sturm* and *Trupp*. The overall message to be conveyed was that the *Leibstandarte* was a creature apart, something special.

The Wehrmacht (Army) kept up its sniping against the *Leibstandarte*. One of the criticisms levelled at Hitler's Guard by the Wehrmacht – and, indeed, at other sections of the SS-VT – was that undue emphasis was given to racial matters and ceremonial trappings, with a consequent neglect of essential military training. Members of the Black Guard were contemptuously dubbed 'asphalt soldiers' because of their propensity for parade-ground marching.

Right: In January 1937, men of the *Leibstandarte* on a parade in celebration of what the Nazis declared to be the 700th anniversary of the founding of Berlin. The sound of their marching is being recorded for radio.

At first, there was much truth in these criticisms. Indeed, they were taken extremely seriously by Himmler, signalled by his action in November 1938 of accepting a retired Lieutenant-General named Paul Hausser from the Wehrmacht into the SS. Hausser was assigned with powers to lick the SS-VT into shape. Gottlieb Berger headed a refurbished Recruiting Office which soon performed with conspicuously more success than the *Allgemeine-SS* (General SS). Seventeen Recruiting Stations, one in each military area, together with the SS Recruiting Office in Berlin, which was enlarged and re-staffed, began the task of finding manpower. Within eight months, Berger's men attracted some 32,000 recruits, most of them drawn from the *Hitler Jugend* (Hitler Youth).

In the early days, the typical candidate for membership was between the ages of 19 and 22, drawn for

Above: In matters of deportment and drill, discipline was draconian within *Leibstandarte* ranks. Men like these at the Lichterfelde barracks were encouraged to consider themselves the chosen ones, and members of an elite.

the most part from the working or the lower middle classes. The results are aptly summarised by Gerald Reitlinger: 'Under the influence of Hausser's cadet schools the *Waffen-SS* was to develop the most efficient of all the military training systems of the Second World War, a cross between the Spartan Hoplites and the Guards Depot at Caterham. It was in fact a joint product of Himmler's dreamy studies of military orders and Hausser's hard practical experience of the Prussian army.'

Hausser was not the only man to have such experience. There was also Felix Steiner, who had served as a junior infantry officer in World War I. As such, he had observed mass ranks of troops who had gone over the top to end up as cannon fodder. Such slaughter and waste of manpower were outmoded. Instead, there must now be elite, highly mobile troops, trained in individual, responsibly planned military teamwork. Above all, Steiner believed in troops gaining high standards of physical fitness before going anywhere near the exercise yard or parade ground. Steiner's emphasis on athletics and cross-country runs at first attracted the scorn of the *Leibstandarte*, until they were faced with colleagues in full kit who could cover 3km (1.8 miles) in 20 minutes. His reforms would soon permeate the entire SS hierarchy.

TRAINING ROUTINE

The training was vigorous, with the day beginning normally enough with reveille at 0600 hours and an hour's pre-breakfast limbering up. Then there was weapon training, interrupted three times a week by a lecture on the life of the Führer, the ideology of National Socialism or the philosophy of racial selection. Compulsory reading included Alfred Rosenberg's *Myth of the Twentieth Century* and Walter Darre's *Im Blud und Boden*.

The emphasis of training exercises was maximum realism, with live ammunition and artillery fire. The reasons for this, as outlined by Himmler, 'was so that every man became accustomed to his weapons and also to being 50–70 metres [160–230ft] of explosion of his own artillery fire'. Predictably, there were casualties, the numbers of which drew criticism, which did not seem to bother the *Reichsführer-SS* unduly. Granted, it was 'a shame to lose each good German lad [but] every drop of blood in peacetime saved streams of blood in battle'. Felix Steiner put it more crudely: a trained *Leibstandarte* man 'would by blows of lightning rapidity split the enemy into fragments and then destroy the dislocated remains'.

War saw the growth of specialist training schools such as the SS Artillery School at Glau and the SS Panzer Grenadier School at Keinschlag. Special training for NCOs was provided at training centres such as the *SS-und-Waffen Unterführerschule Lauenburg.*

Relations between the recruits and their instructors from the Wehrmacht were uneasy at first, but soon improved. Albert Stenwedel, a recruit who ultimately joined 1st Company, *Leibstandarte SS Adolf Hitler* and trained at the Zossen troops training grounds, south of Berlin, recalled:

'We received our military training from the non-commissioned officers of the 8th Infantry Regiment, a unit of the 100,000-man army from Silesia. We received excellent training and drill, field and guard duty, which formed the foundation of our career as soldiers … Our instructors were long-serving career soldiers who remained completely neutral politically. The recruits were all stalwart SS men who experienced the political struggle and who knew unemployment, hard times and persecution. All this was rather foreign to our instructors. After just a week of working together there was already a close comradeship between us which could scarcely have been better. My instructor, *Unterfeldwebel* Reigber, even invited me to his wedding, and I was happy to take part.'

Discipline, though, was never relaxed. The *Leibstandarte* man was expected to go on leave with a handkerchief folded with a designated number of creases. If a paybook produced an unsightly bulge in a uniform pocket, then the wearer could be deprived of his pay.

'BAND OF BROTHERS'

The training schools produced the basis for a hard, heartless fighting animal, but this tells only half the story. Among officers, NCOs and other ranks, a sense of fellowship and mutual respect was ongoing. The conception of the future *Waffen-SS* as a 'band of brothers' extended to comparatively minor matters. In the Wehrmacht, for example, it was mandatory for the men to secure their lockers to prevent theft. For Himmler's men, no such practice was allowed. In rare cases of theft, the prosecution of the individual concerned was regarded solely as a private matter and handled without reference to any outside authority. As an indication of Sepp Dietrich's style, he frequently ate meals in the company of his men, rather than with

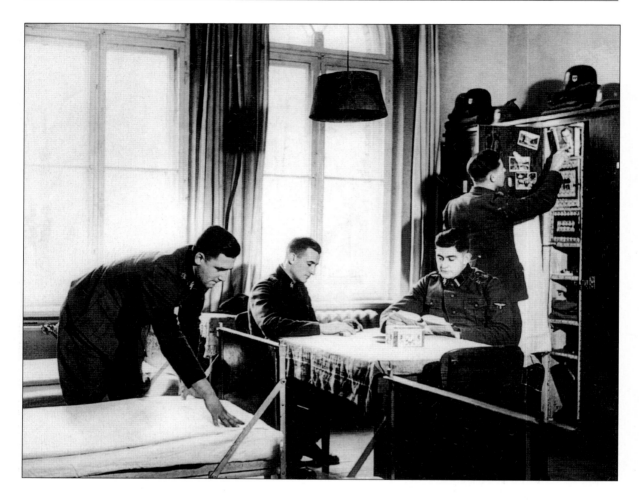

Above: As this obviously posed picture is intended to demonstrate, even when off duty, the *Leibstandarte* had to maintain the highest standards. This extended to keeping their quarters spartan and spotless.

his fellow senior officers. Overall, there was a form of democracy quite unknown in the Wehrmacht. This was at complete variance with the rigid class-consciousness which had long being a characteristic of the Prussian military tradition, a tradition which, it must be added, survived in some other branches of the armed SS.

This breaking down of social and professional barriers between officers and men had its origins in World War I, which had seen the formation of the *Sturmabteilungen*, or Storm Troopers, whose character differed considerably from that of the remainder of the German Army. Like the later SS, the sense of superiority among the *Sturmabteilungen*

bordered on the arrogant; here, they had proclaimed to lesser mortals, was an elite. Certainly, they were more privileged, received higher quality rations, were excused much of the tedium of trench warfare and had enjoyed enhanced rest and leave. The inheritance of the *Sturmabteilungen*, however much resented by their fellows, was to prove a significant and valuable advantage when it came to the Russian battlefields in the 1940s; it became com-

monplace for officers of senior field rank to lead combat groups in all-out assaults.

The equality ethos was obtained from the very start of entry into the training schools by would-be *Leibstandarte* young men. For officers, the armed SS was a career open to talent, rather than birthright. In their history of the *Leibstandarte*, which devotes considerable space to unit character (see bibliography), James Lucas and Matthew Cooper write:

'Before 1938, 40 per cent of the SS-officer cadets had only received elementary school education and, whereas in the armed forces 49 per cent of the officers were of military families, the proportion was only 5 per cent in the SS-VT. Likewise in the

Above: Ideology was a cornerstone of the *Leibstandarte's* indoctrination of its young volunteers, who were required to attend classes on the main tenets of National Socialism, as well as the philosophy of racial selection.

Wehrmacht, less than 2 per cent were of peasant stock, whereas 90 per cent of SS-VT commanders had been brought up on the land. (This, incidentally, reflects the high proportion of recruits which came from the countryside rather than from the towns – in some parts of Germany as many as a third of the farmers' sons joined the ranks of the armed SS — the same areas which gave the greatest support to the NSDAP.)'

Left: Another face of the *Leibstandarte*: 'Hitler's own' amid flowers and smiles. This photograph, taken in Berlin on 20 April 1937, shows the crowds gathering to watch a parade to mark the Führer's birthday.

Perfection in discipline and training, however desirable, was not the only characteristic of the *Leibstandarte*. As in all of the SS, Nazi ideology fuelled every initiative. A weekly indoctrination session was mandatory for each *Leibstandarte* man. Its permanent education officer declared: 'Its main point is to influence the *Leibstandarte* so that it can at any time be the shock troops of the regime in ideological studies ... It must recognise no other ties than to the Führer and his orders ... We must and can so use the time ... to weld the units of the *Leibstandarte* together and make them into a stout tool in the hand of the Führer.'

ORGANISATION

Authors James Lucas and Matthew Cooper record the events of October 1933, which provided one instance among many of the conflict between the *Leibstandarte* (to all intents and purposes, Adolf Hitler) and Himmler, sensitive as ever to what might be seen as even the smallest encroachment on his authority. By that date, the *Leibstandarte* was made up of a staff, two SS *Sturmbanne* (battalions), each consisting of three SS *Stürme* (companies or units) and one signals *Zug* (platoon).

The following year the unit was renamed *SS Standarte 1-Leibstandarte Adolf Hitler*, the first of what was intended to be a series of SS formations. Hitler, however, was not attracted to the idea of featureless numbers for his elite. Thus, by the middle of 1934, the various components as we have seen, received such designations as *Bataillon* and *Kompanie*.

Thereafter, expansion grew apace up to the eve of war. By May 1935, the *Leibstandarte*, a motorised regiment comprising 2660 men, represented more than a quarter of the total strength of the SS-VT. The following July, the trench mortar company (No. 13) had become an infantry gun company, followed by that of an armoured car platoon. By September 1939, the number of men had increased to 3700

and, by the following May, the *Leibstandarte* had an additional infantry gun company, a lightweight infantry column and an artillery battalion which was made up of three batteries.

Further enhancement of the prestige of the SS-VT had already been provided by large-scale exercises at the Munsterlager manoeuvre centre, in the presence of handpicked generals who had expressed scepticism of the capability of SS troops. It was a full-scale combat exercise, prepared by Himmler and commanded by Felix Steiner. Richard Schulze-Kossens, who was to serve with *Leibstandarte* in three campaigns, was present and, after the war, recalled the exercises for a British television documentary, *To the Death's Head True*: 'The whole regiment was under fire from artillery, infantry, marksmen, submachine guns, hand grenades and flame-throwers. That had never been done in the German Army before, and you can only do that sort of thing with volunteers who have been particularly well trained.'

The Führer's commitment to armed SS troops appeared set in stone. Any objections from the Wehrmacht were thrust aside; no matter the opposition, the SS-VT would now be organised as a division. The exigencies of war, however, temporarily threw this out of kilter, following Hitler's decision to invade Poland. Drafts from the *Leibstandarte*, *Deutschland* and *Germania* were placed piecemeal under Wehrmacht command. Only at the cessation of the Balkan campaign was the unit officially designated SS Division *Leibstandarte Adolf Hitler*.

UNIFORM AND INSIGNIA

Consistency was not a strong characteristic of any echelon of the *Waffen-SS*, especially when it came to dress. Under war conditions, it became impossible, largely due to shortage of material and to the profusion of items introduced over the years.

The pre-war uniform of the SS-VT was made up of a single-breasted tunic with four aluminium buttons down the front, pleated and buttoned breast pockets and sloping button-down hip pockets. Black trousers were tucked into standard black Wehrmacht-pattern marching boots (jackboots), while a black cap or steel helmet – as well as black leather belts with SS buckles – were worn.

As might be expected of an elite formation, the *Leibstandarte* uniform incorporated notable differences. Dietrich's biographer Charles Messenger was told by Sepp's eldest son, Wolf-Dieter, that his father had been responsible for the design. As he rose in rank and prestige – Commander of the Leibstandarte, 1st SS Panzer Corps and 6th SS Panzer Army – Dietrich displayed a degree of licence. Unique to him was use of a standard army general's service cap with gold chin cord and gold piping, rather than the standard SS silver piping. The cap was worn with the silver SS death's head emblem on the band, while the SS national emblem was hand embroidered in gold wire. The national emblem and the Adolf Hitler cuff title were on Dietrich's field blouses and greatcoats in gold embroidered letters and borders on the standard black background. Similar elegance extended to a greatcoat of gold hand-embroidered insignia and was of field-grey doeskin material with green satin lining.

Only *Leibstandarte* members were permitted to wear white accoutrements with their black uniform; in addition, the SS runes on the studs of the collar bore no unit number. The SS collar patches worn by Dietrich's men were a clue to rank – insignia was worn on the left for ranks up to and including *SS-Obersturmbannführer*, on both sides for more senior officers. Members of the *Leibstandarte* were in fact distinguishable from other SS by their dress in a number of ways. The 28mm (1.1in) wide armband of black tape carried the inscription 'Adolf Hitler' in German script and was worn around the top of the left cuff. The LAH monogram was carried on the shoulder straps. Service or uniform caps consisted of a peak with field-grey cover, black cap band and a black leather peak or visor. The SS version of the national emblem (the eagle) in matt silver was worn on the cap and on the upper left sleeve. On the front silver of the cap band was featured a matt silver SS *Totenkopf* (Death's head). In 1935, an earthgrey service dress which had been issued to the *Leibstandarte* with its swastika brassard, black service

cap and black breeches had been replaced by a fieldgrey uniform similar to that worn by the Wehrmacht. Indeed, from 1938 until the war's end, the final form of service uniform for the armed SS was Wehrmacht dress.

With the war looming, the armoured units were issued in 1938 with a black uniform. This was for severely practical reasons: black lessened the visibility of grease and dirt. Special clothing designed for easy movement within tanks and armoured cars was similar to that of the Wehrmacht. When the title *Waffen-SS* was adopted in 1940, members of the *Leibstandarte* formations received the standard army-pattern field-grey tunics with five buttons down the front and patch pockets on the hips, as well as the chest. In 1941 came identically cut fieldgrey for assault-gun crews and, subsequently, selfpropelled anti-tank units. As the war progressed, there was inevitably a wide variety of multipurpose camouflage designs, all of them intended to fit in with the appropriate season. Thus a single outer garment could be donned throughout the year as it was reversible – one side largely green for summer wear, the other in warm brown shades for the rest of the year.

LOYALTY UNTO DEATH

Symbolism played its part in the design of *Waffen-SS* uniform and insignia. Notably – and not exclusive to the *Leibstandarte* – there was the Death's Head badge which, worn upon the cap, signified loyalty unto death. The double-slashed *Sig* rune, or victory rune, on the right collar evoked victory, rather than, as is often supposed, the letters SS for *Schutzstaffel*.

One indication of how the gap between the *Waffen-SS* and the Wehrmacht narrowed with the approach of war – in particular, with significance to the *Leibstandarte* – was the issue of shoulder boards for officers of general rank. As Stan Cook and

Right: Although their duties were largely ceremonial before the war, members of the *Leibstandarte* were expected to know how to handle a weapon. This recruit is shown receiving instruction on his Mauser rifle.

R. James Bender point out in their history of the *Leibstandarte*, with its exhaustive study of uniforms and insignia, the use of shoulder boards was yet another example of the strictly hierarchical structure of the *Waffen-SS*.

In the matter of army-style shoulder boards, there was reluctance to extend to the armed SS permission to wear these. It was late in November 1939 that *Gruppenführer* Paul Hausser of *Leibstandarte* and *Gruppenführer* Theodore Eicke of *Totenkopf* were permitted to use them. A year later, the use of dual rank was introduced. Officers who held the equivalent general rank were permitted to append the title to their SS rank: *SS-Brigadeführer und Generalmajor der Waffen-SS*; *SS-Gruppenführer und Generalleutnant der Waffen-SS*; and *SS-Obergruppenführer und General der Waffen-SS*.

An indication of an officer's branch of service was the use of colour (*Farbe*), introduced to the armed SS on the brink of war. *Waffenfarbe* was employed as pip-

Above: These recruits in Berlin in late 1938 are undergoing training for promotion to officer rank within the *Leibstandarte*. Attendance was compulsory at regular indoctrination sessions conducted by an education officer.

ing or underlay, or shoulder straps and cords for all ranks up to *SS-Brigadeführer*.

WAGNER

Music formed an important part of *Leibstandarte* ceremonial. In August 1933, the music platoon was formed by its first and only director, *SS-Hauptsturmführer* Herman Müller-John, who enjoyed the official title *Leibstandarten-Obermusikmeister*. He was in charge of 36 musicians for the band, a number which grew to 64 within three years. Before the war, the band travelled throughout Germany performing in concert and was a highlight of the 1936 Berlin Olympic Games. Hitler's devotion to Wagner's music was well known and it was scarcely surprising that, each year, the band furnished a brass ensemble at the Wagner festival in Bayreuth. On 1 October 1938, the *Leibstandarte*, in conjunction with the Wehrmacht, went to the Sudeten territory of Czechoslovakia to mark Hitler's visit to inspect his new conquests. The Führer was greeted in the town of Horsin by the *Leibstandarte* music corps playing the regimental march and the *Badenweiler Marsch*, one of Hitler's favourites. In addition, the music corps played regularly outside the Reich Chancellery and at a number of party functions.

The centrepiece of the band – indeed, of many German military bands – was the *Schellenbaum* or 'Jingling Johnnie', referring to the plenitude of bells. The *Schellenbaum* served as the standard of the band and, in the case of the *Leibstandarte*, was patterned

Above: A *Leibstandarte* colour party in the shade of a giant Nazi eagle during a rally before the war. Like their armbands, their standards were a source of great pride to the men of the *Leibstandarte*.

after a version which had been used by the German Imperial Army. The inevitable eagle topped a panel with an eagle and swastika, and the words '*Adolf Hitler-Standarte*'. Another swastika also appeared on an eight-pointed silver star above the standard half-moon carrying yet again the name of the unit.

The black velvet banners used on fanfare trumpets of the SS were usually of the same general design as the original ones for the *Leibstandarte*, measuring 42cm by 42cm (16.5in by 16.5in). On one side was a *Totenkopf* (Death's Head) about 23cm (9in) in height, and below it were the words '*Adolf Hitler-Standarte*', in a modified Gothic script and measuring approximately 5cm (2in) in height. On the other side were the SS runes bordered with a 1cm (0.39in) long fringe of aluminium and the top was attached to the trumpet. The *Totenkopf* and '*Adolf Hitler-Standarte*' insignia also accompanied the kettle drum used in ceremonial.

STANDARDS AND PENNANTS

Reference has already been made to the Congress of Victory rally to celebrate Hitler's assumption of power. On 1 September, a lone SS man mounted the platform to display the *Blütfahne* (blood banner). This was, an outstanding example of Nazi symbolism, since the banner derived its name from allegedly having been drenched in the gore of the Nazi martyrs killed during the abortive Beer Hall Putsch. From then on, at each Nuremburg rally held, Hitler would consecrate new party colours by touching them with one hand, while with the other he grasped the cloth of the bullet-ridden *Blütfahne*.

The 1933 rally was of particular importance to the *Leibstandarte*. Here it was presented with its double-sided, rectangular standard with its field of red silk, edged with a wool fringe in black, white and red. One inscription read '*NAT.SOZ.DEUTSCHE ARBEITER-PARTEI*' and another '*STURMABTEILUNG*'. Below the standard's carrying pole with its wreath and swastika was a metal box which formed part of the pole and was inscribed 'Adolf Hitler'. In the same year, the *Leibstandarte* was also presented with its first battalion flags with their striking red fields and large white circle to contain the swastika. A patch

embroidered in aluminium wire carried the number of the battalion in Roman numerals and, in the case of the *Leibstandarte*, a slant bar and runes. The following year, Himmler presented the *Leibstandarte* with a series of new flags, as well as a new standard.

NEW COLOURS

The year 1940 was particularly eventful for the *Leibstandarte* in terms of the presentation of new regimental colours, notably in Metz, France, on 7 September, where the unit also received three new-style infantry battalion colours and three guidons (pennants) for the artillery units. These guidons were the possessions of mobile, notably artillery, units and were intended to be flown from moving vehicles. Here, again, we can detect the insidious influence of the Wehrmacht within the *Waffen-SS*. Thus, at the outbreak of war, the *Leibstandarte* ceased using the usual SS pennants and switched to the Wehrmacht style.

Identification insignia on vehicles underwent change throughout the war and, on some occasions, were dispensed with altogether for security reasons — for example, during the French campaign of May 1940. The most celebrated insignia was that of the key. Introduced in 1941, it was based upon the word 'Dietrich' (skeleton key). Here symbolism played its part: the *Dietrich* would unlock any door, including that of triumph over the enemy.

Cook and Bender explain that, at first, the Baltic Cross (*Baltenkreuz*) was proposed for the first tactical vehicle insignia. This was already worn on the uniform of Wilhelm Trabandt, the 3rd Battalion Commander, who objected to his personal decoration being used as a vehicle symbol and proposed the *Dietrich* instead. Its use quickly spread to the entire regiment and was also used on aircraft carrying out observation for the *Leibstandarte*.

Incidentally, the *Dietrich*, which had several variants to its design, was embellished with oak leaves when

Left: *Obergruppenführer* Sepp Dietrich inspects his men of the *Leibstandarte* as they present arms during a ceremony to mark the third anniversary of the division's foundation at the Lichterfelde barracks.

Sepp Dietrich himself was awarded the Oak Leaves to his Knight's Cross.

WEAPONS, PERSONNEL AND EQUIPMENT

Although the exigencies of war demanded that most of the differences and rivalries between the army and the armed SS be put on hold, one bone of contention remained: the claim that units of the *Waffen-SS* (the term 'SS-VT' was dropped in 1939) became better equipped than Wehrmacht formations. Arguments for and against this point of view still rage to this day among military historians. They point out that, up to 1940, the Wehrmacht steadily refused to surrender any of its heavy artillery to the SS. It was not until March that three heavy (150mm (5.91in)) artillery battalions were organised, one for each frontline division, together with a light (105mm (4.13in)) battalion for the *Leibstandarte*.

In terms of personnel, however, growing strength for Himmler's legions could be traced to a Führer decree of 17 August 1938, which laid down that, in time of war, the armed SS would be reinforced by the *Totenkopfverbände* (Death's Head formations which included concentration camp guards). By 1940, there were four SS divisions: the *Leibstandarte Adolf Hitler*, *Reich*, *Totenkopf* and *Polizei*, plus the nucleus of a fifth, *Viking*. The *Leibstandarte* went into the war with 3700 men in four infantry battalions with supporting, 75mm (2.96in) infantry gun and 37mm (1.45in) anti-tank companies, plus a pioneer and a motorcycle reconnaissance platoon.

On 6 August, Hitler authorised the expansion of the *Leibstandarte* to brigade strength. Within days, its title had been slightly altered to *Leibstandarte SS Adolf Hitler*, with the addition of an artillery regiment, a pioneer battalion, a signals company and a reconnaissance detachment.

The strength included: I–III Battalions, each of three rifle, one machine-gun and one heavy company – the latter consisting of two anti-tank gun platoons (37mm (1.45in) Pak) and one each of mortars (80mm (3.15in)) and pioneers; IV Heavy Battalion of one light infantry-gun company (75mm (2.96in)), one heavy infantry-gun company (75mm (2.96in)), one anti-tank gun company (47mm (1.85in) self-propelled), one field-gun company (75mm (2.96in) self-propelled) and one anti-aircraft gun company (37mm (1.45in)); and V Guard Battalion of four companies stationed at Berlin-Lichterfelde. There were also one reconnaissance detachment, one artillery regiment, one pioneer battalion and one signals detachment. As the Balkans campaign finally drew to a close, the unit was officially given the designation SS Division *Leibstandarte Adolf Hitler*.

Some idea of its growing power can be gathered from the fact that, by the end of 1942, the *Leibstandarte* had reached a strength of 678 officers and 20,166 other ranks. By the time the unit received its final title of 1st SS Panzer Division *Leibstandarte* in October 1943, it took as many as around 150 trains to move the entire division – minus its armour – from the East to Italy. By June of the following year, *Leibstandarte* was made up of 21,386 men, armed with 45 self-propelled guns and 50 Mark IV, 38 Mark V and 29 Mark VI tanks.

The *Leibstandarte* received generous quantities of the latest and best equipment and, in its heyday, it was organised as one of the strongest six or seven German divisions of World War II. James Lucas writes: 'In late 1943, for example, the *Leibstandarte* was sent 22 Tiger tanks at a time when Germany's total was only 74 … The *Leibstandarte*'s last battles took enormous toll of its strength at a time when no adequate reinforcements were forthcoming. The situation was so bad that, on 7 April 1945, Hitler's Guard was down to a mere 57 officers, 229 NCOs, 1296 men and 16 tanks in the field.'

The strengths of the *Leibstandarte* in both numbers and men – as well as in equipment – was to vary greatly throughout the World War II. This was due to its reorganisations, but as the war progressed, it was also a result of shortages of material and the increasingly heavy losses suffered at the front line.

Right: In March 1938, men of the *Leibstandarte* accompanied panzer units into Austria where their reception in Vienna was ecstatic. The *Schellenbaum* ('Jingling Johnny') was used by many German military bands.

CHAPTER THREE

BLOODING

The invasion of Poland was sparked by Hitler's order of 31 August 1939. The next day, Stukas, panzers and infantry struck across the frontier at dawn. Here was the birth of a new sort of war: the *Blitzkrieg*, or 'lightning war', in which the *Leibstandarte* was soon to take part.

His hold on Austria and Czechoslovakia secured, Hitler turned his attention to Poland, his next intended target for conquest. Hitler's deep-seated hatred of Poland was inherited. As early as 1922, General Hans von Seeckt, regarded as the 'father' of the *Reichswehr*, had declared: 'Poland's existence is intolerable, incompatible with the essential conditions of German life. Poland must and will go.'

By diktat of the peacemakers of Versailles, the German province of East Prussia on the Baltic Sea had been separated from the rest of the Reich by a corridor which gave Poland its sole access at Danzig (Gdansk). On 21 March 1939, the Führer turned up the heat: Danzig must be restored to Germany, which must have the freedom to build road and rail links to East Prussia across Polish territory. As was to be expected, Poland refused. The war clouds began to gather.

Hitler, however, seeking freedom to act against Poland, still shared a fear that had long haunted German military thinking: the spectre of fighting a war on two fronts. This was relieved by the signing of

Left: Polish Foreign Minister Josef Beck shakes hands with the commander of a *Leibstandarte* honour guard welcoming him to Berlin on 3 July 1935. Just over four years later, the unit would take part in the invasion of Poland.

the Nazi–Soviet Pact during the night of 23 August 1939. Nazi Foreign Minister Joachim von Ribbentrop and his Soviet counterpart, Vyacheslav Molotov, put their signatures to a 10-year non-aggression pact, cemented by an agreement that Poland should be conquered and then divided. For the Poles, it was a death knell.

INVASION

As early as April 1939, *Oberkommando der Wehrmacht* (OKW) had issued its Directive for the Uniform Preparation for War in 1939/40. After some delay, Hitler gave his armies the final signal for invasion at dawn on 1 September. One of the most significant passages of the OKW directive had stated that the destruction of the Polish Army would be carried out through surprise attack. This was a sign that here was the start, not simply of a conflict, but of a new sort of war. Clausewitz, the German military theorist, many of whose pronouncements had been hitherto regarded as holy writ, had proclaimed over a century before: 'Blood is the price of victory. Philanthropists may easily imagine that there is a skilful method of disarming and overcoming the enemy without great bloodshed and that this is the proper tendency of the Art of War ... That is an error that must be extirpated.'

But this was 1939, the era of *Blitzkrieg*, or lightning war, with victories being delivered not in rivers of blood, but in tactics of speed and shock delivered with all the resources of new technology. The battlefield would belong to highly mobile forces, to the Panzers, their divisions thrusting deep into any enemy's defences and cutting up troops into separate pockets. Before that would come bombing cover from screaming Stuka dive-bombers.

The start of the blitz invasion of Poland, which was designated *Case Weiss* (Case White), found the Poles under attack from three separate directions. In the north of the country, General Fedor von Bock's 4th Army attacked from Pomerania in the west, while his 3rd Army came from East Prussia, in a giant pincer movement. The aim was to cut off the Polish corridor at its tip. Then came the swing south to attack Warsaw. Still further south, under General von Rundstedt, the 8th and 10th armies struck east from Silesia for Warsaw, while 14th pushed east for Cracow (Kraków) and Lwow (Lvov).

MASSIVE FORCES

The German muscle appeared impressive. In the east alone were to be positioned 27 infantry divisions, six Panzer divisions, four light divisions and one cavalry brigade. Another 16 divisions were to be created on mobilisation. But all was not entirely well – not least because of opposition among the more hidebound sections of the Wehrmacht, who distrusted with a sneer the 'tank troops' with their pretensions of technical superiority. Expansion of the army had taken place over just four years and the supply of equipment, particularly to the Panzer divisions, had been deficient: tanks were equipped with machine guns rather than cannon. Against that, though, was superiority in the large number of independently operating armoured and motorised units. The unknown factor was how they would conduct themselves in battle.

The extension of German territory which had been brought about by the occupation of Czechoslovakia dangerously exposed the southern flank of Poland. The Polish army, with an instinct for trouble, had increased its army's infantry strength

Right: Target practice before the invasion of Poland in 1939. At this stage of the war the *Leibstandarte* and other *Waffen-SS* units relied heavily on the Wehrmacht for their uniforms and equipment.

from 30 to 39 divisions. All other units had been reinforced; the air force had been reorganised with a bomber brigade and a pursuit brigade. Plans were in place for the bulk of the armed forces to be mobilised within 72 hours.

But it was a case of too little, too late. The 400 aircraft of the Polish front line were largely obsolete. A motorised force of 225 modern tanks included 80 obsolete ones. In a scarcely better state were its 534 reconnaissance carriers and 100 armoured cars of obsolete types. Only one of the 12 cavalry brigades was armoured, and the artillery did not compare favourably in calibre or range with its German counterpart either.

As early as the middle of June, the *Leibstandarte*, which had returned to the Berlin area two months previously, had received its orders. *Sommerübung* (summer exercise) called for combat readiness by 1 August 1939. In preparation for their first blooding in battle, Sepp Dietrich's men moved out of Lichterfelde, leaving behind a sprinkling of reserve, training and security troops. They arrived in the assembly area around Hundsfeld-Kunersdorf, north of Breslau, with an injunction from Himmler ringing in their ears: 'SS men, I expect you to do more than your duty.' In captivity after the war, Dietrich was frank: 'The Führer's order was to kill without mercy the entire Polish race. We were the Führer's men. We had our order. We pressed ahead.'

The battle experience of this former NCO had been in the infinitely different environment of World War I. Up to the invasion of Poland, all had been but theory: attending courses for motorised regimental commanders at Zossen and for Panzer division commanders at the tank school at Winsdorf. Dietrich was now faced with an apprenticeship in this new war, encouraged by the fact that during the previous June, Hitler had finally railroaded the vocal critics within the army and declared that the SS-VT would be

Above: A *Leibstandarte* reconnaissance team at the outset of the invasion of Poland in September 1939. They are armed with a mixture of weapons: from left to right, a Kar 98K rifle, and a MP38 and a MP28 machine pistol.

organised as a division. An artillery regiment had been raised at Juterborg with drafts from the *Leibstandarte, Deutschland* and *Germania.*

Leibstandarte was part of Army Group South. Von Rundstedt, as group commander, soon found work for Dietrich's men under the control of 17th Infantry Division. Since there was a lack of reconnaissance strength for the left wing of the 10th Army, Dietrich's men filled this need, acting as the link between 8th and 10th armies, under the commands of Generals Johannes Blaskowitz and Walter von Reichenau.

The first task of the *Leibstandarte,* approaching from the vicinity of Breslau, centred on a key height lying behind the Prosna River, which lay on the path from Breslau where there was a fortified frontier line. It faced several echelons of Polish infantry and artillery. Adrenaline ran high within 8th Army with the commencement of hostilities at 0045 hours on 1 September. Just before the start, some newly enlisted men who had not yet been able to recite the *Leibstandarte* oath of loyalty were ordered to do so before moving into battle. These were fresh-faced young SS men, virgins among what all too soon would be killing fields. One of their number had already written home:

'I am writing this by very poor light … Today we shall be at war with Poland unless the Poles see sense. Tomorrow I shall be a complete soldier. Personal thoughts I have expelled from my mind; only one single thought remains – Germany.'

Advance was speedy: some five or eight kilometres (three or four miles) within 75 minutes. The *Leibstandarte* reached the German–Polish border at 0445 hours and the first crossing took place at Gola, where the bridge over the Prosna was seized, breasted by the SS troops in the face of easily overcome opposition from the Polish 10th Infantry Division with their 37mm (1.49in) guns. Ahead lay Boleslavecz and, beyond it, Wieuroszov, the town where the *Leibstandarte* was to link up with the 17th Infantry Division on its left. Attempts to halt the advance proved costly for the Poles; by 1000 hours, Boleslavecz was in German hands and there were columns of prisoners in their field grey, the Eagle of Poland shining in the welt of their field caps.

The countryside, much of it dense birch forests, had concealed Poles with machine guns who knew their own territory well; there were dismounted attacks on the long columns of *Leibstandarte* vehicles. At the end of the day, however, Dietrich's men had swept up all their objectives: 10th, 17th and 25th Polish Infantry Divisions, together with those of the Wielpolska and Wolwyska Cavalry Brigades. These men had fought hard counterattacking, often hand-to-hand. One *Leibstandarte* man recalled: 'They came into the attack in long lines, not quite shoulder-to-shoulder but very close together. They had a battle cry – a long drawn-out hurrah and we could also hear the officers shouting.' First German casualties – the overall count was seven killed and 20 wounded – had included the crew of an armed reconnaissance car, victims of a Polish mine.

THE ATTACK CONTINUES

The link-up with 17th Infantry Division was to be followed by an assault on the Warta River in the vicinity of Burzenin. A six-man machine-gun crew from 1st Company *Leibstandarte* was ordered across a partially blown wooden bridge to the other side of the river to report on the likely strength of opposition. One of the crew later recalled the sudden, totally unexpected appearance of Sepp Dietrich in forage cap, his insignia of rank concealed by a motorcyclist's long coat. As the men moved towards the bridge, Dietrich himself followed, passing disassembled machine-gun barrels and ammunition canisters. Before melting into the darkness, he called out with a chuckle: 'Good luck and don't be afraid. You're not going to drown, just get a wet arse.'

But it was not a happy experience for the *Leibstandarte*, who encountered resistance both from enemy firepower and the sandy soil which held up its vehicles. Another blow to the men's pride was the knowledge that elements of 10th Army were already crossing the river. It was not until late on 4 September that the crossing was finally made in its entirety.

Casualties by now were mounting, which did little for the morale and, just as seriously, the discipline of the *Leibstandarte*. Major General Loch, commanding 17th Infantry Division, complained of wild firing by the *Leibstandarte* and a propensity for torching every village during its progress. It was made clear that such a practice was objected to on strict military operational considerations, not sentiment. Burning villages held up the tempo of the tactics of fire and movement, as well as depriving the troops of shelter when it was needed. Still, advance there was by the young volunteers, with the Poles being swept up before them. The riposte to the *Leibstandarte* was vicious, due to the combined Polish forces of 30th Infantry Division, 21st Infantry Regiment and the armoured cars of Wolwyska Cavalry Brigade.

FURIOUS RESISTANCE

The *Leibstandarte* moved on towards the town of Wieuroszov, where the Poles attacked using every scrap of cover, including every bush which seemed to serve as a machine-gun cover. With his fellows, one member of 1st Company ran into a knot of Poles clad in civilian trousers beneath their army coats, their refuge a grain field. But the advance was unstoppable: 10th Army achieved a breakthrough north of Chestakova. Units from two panzer divisions pressed their advantage between the Lodz and Kraków armies, storming across the Pilica River on the headlong thrust towards Warsaw.

The next 8th Army objective was Lodz, with its heavily defended approaches. Two *Leibstandarte* companies, 1st and 2nd, encountered stiff opposition and suffered heavy casualties, despite tank support. Polish anti-tank fire prevented the advance of the panzers; units were ordered to disengage from the Poles so that the artillery could conduct fire preparatory to a fresh attack. By 1800 hours on 7 September, despite outnumbering the Germans, the Poles had been overwhelmed and had abandoned the town. The next target was Pabianice, a small market town and road–rail junction on the river, where the Poles succeeded in keeping at bay *Leibstandarte*'s 1st Battalion. The battalion, supported by another from 23rd Panzer Regiment, made little headway beyond the town's western outskirts.

This particular engagement provided another instance of the advantages that the defenders enjoyed on their own territory. Well-camouflaged Polish riflemen had the marksmanship skills of huntsmen, well used to taking up positions in trees and picking off the enemy below. The *Leibstandarte*'s countermeasures included raking trees and bushes with rifle fire and lobbed grenades. This was also an area of vast fields of sunflowers and maize; men on both sides took to stalking one another through the tall plants. There were some ingenious instances of camouflage. One *Leibstandarte* man reported:

'The Poles are devilishly cunning … They had dugouts with crops growing on the roof and were almost invisible and hard to detect. We had to stalk them like characters from a Karl May Wild West novel. When we found a dug-out we blew it up with bundles of

Below: An armoured car involved in the fighting for Sochaczew, west of Warsaw. The white cross insignia common to all armour in the Polish campaign was later changed to a less conspicuous black.

grenades. Some of them may have been linked by tunnels; a combat report had mentioned this ... We captured more than 50 and it took us hours before we had wiped out this nest ...'

The Poles were also helped by reinforcements from those who had originally withdrawn in the face of 10th Army's advance. These men were able to launch fierce counterattacks, at one point even threatening Dietrich's own headquarters, before an entire infantry regiment was sent to his aid.

Early progress by the *Leibstandarte* was successful, but it was forced to detour from the advance on Pabianice, which was heavily defended. 'Hitler's own' suffered the indignity of being extricated from this danger spot by the intervention of Infantry Regiment 55 of the 10th Division. By the early hours of the 8th, Pabianice had fallen, but *Leibstandarte* received scant kudos for this achieved objective. Major General Loch redoubled his criticism: the training and conduct of the SS men had been shown to be severely deficient. Rescue measures in such circumstances could not be afforded. The *Leibstandarte* constituted a liability, therefore it should be withdrawn into reserve. Although this did not happen, even so, it *was* removed from 8th Army and sent to Georg-Hans Reinhardt's 4th Panzer Division in von Reichenau's 10th Army.

After a move to prevent Polish forces from escaping from an entrapped pocket down the Grodisk–Masczovoc road, south-east of Warsaw, the 1st Battalion moved on to Oltarzev, a town on the way to the Polish capital. The plight of Polish forces was made increasingly perilous by the arrival of the battalion's artillery component. Polish columns perished along with their vehicles under murderous German fire. By now it was evening, and the mist which gathered was made even more of a hazard by the smoke from the guns.

The engagement which followed resembled a tableau from some earlier war, with troops of horse artillery storming out of the smoke. They came straight into the path of the guns, which were soon being turned on columns of civilians who had sought to withdraw safely under the protection of the Polish

Army. But still there was no admission of defeat by the Poles. As one German eyewitness stated: 'They came with their heads held high as if they were swimmers breasting the waves.'

Von Reichenau's 10th Army reeled north, forming a block along the Bzura, west of Warsaw; on the same evening, the *Leibstandarte* joined it on the southwestern outskirts of the capital. The other two divisions took up positions to capture Blonie, east of 1st Battalion and also on the way to the capital. The battle of Warsaw, which the Poles had declared a fortress, was about to begin. With it came the personal control of von Rundstedt himself, with the order that 8th and 10th Armies annihilate all Polish forces that remained between the Bzura and Vistula. Von Reichenau's spearhead reached the outskirts of Warsaw in eight days, having travelled 225km (140 miles). There it halted, a solid, immovable steel door. From East Prussia to the northwest, Guderian's armoured corps arrowed towards Brest-Litovsk, capturing the town on 14 September and making contact with the armour of General Paul Baron von Kleist coming up from the south.

HEAVY LOSSES

The Poles, however, were not ready to admit defeat. They launched counterstrokes; heavy street fighting involved 4th Panzer Division on the outskirts of Warsaw. Although the division's commander, Lieutenant General Georg-Hans Reinhardt, was optimistic that the bulk of Polish resistance had been annihilated, in reality, men had been forced back with heavy losses, including around half their armour. The *Leibstandarte* joined the division and, for the next few days, the two fought together in a bitter battle. For virtually the first time since the 'asphalt soldiers' had relinquished textbook training and blackboard lecturing for the real thing, *Leibstandarte* was on the defensive. The result was the overrunning of 6th Company of the 2nd Battalion and the death of its commander, *Haupsturmführer* Seppel Lange. Strong forces in the Poznan and Pomorze armies launched a counterattack to the south-east across the Bzura River which ran west of Warsaw and into the Vistula.

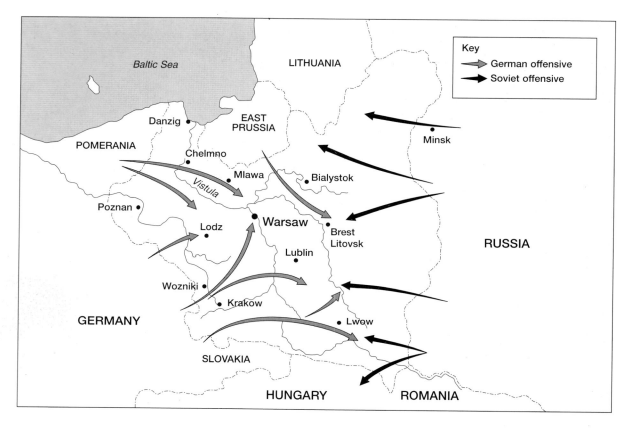

Above: The invasion of Poland in September 1939. The country was first attacked from Germany and East Prussia. The Soviet Union then invaded from the east some weeks later as had been agreed in the Nazi–Soviet Pact.

The German armoured vehicles disregarded the efforts of engineers working desperately to complete bridges, driving headlong down the steep eastern bank into the waters of the Bzura under a storm of Polish artillery. The weather was atrocious; tanks were stuck in muddied exit points and those which made it were puny in number until the arrival of reinforcements.

Lieutenant General Reinhardt's optimism that all serious resistance had been eliminated was premature. There was still the Polish garrison within Warsaw to the east, prepared to resist with everything it had. An attempt on 8/9 September to take the city by assault had come to nothing. German forces then had to withdraw to the Bzura river sector.

VITAL SECTOR

Some idea of the importance that the Germans attached to taking out the sector can be gauged by the fact that von Rundstedt himself took charge of the offensive. A prime role was assigned to 16th Corps, with *Leibstandarte* as an important adjunct. On 14 September came the order to seal off the eastern exit from the Bzura pocket with an attack northwards to the Vistula, a goal not achieved until five days later.

The Polish army faced annihilation. It was clear that Warsaw was a spent force. The path there could only be taken by men rendered exhausted by the forced marches and vicious battles. Their arrival temporarily boosted the morale of those in the capital, but the arrivals were soldiers who had abandoned

Above: The *Leibstandarte* in action in the town of Sochaczew, which, despite enduring heavy bombing and shelling, put up one of the strongest defences against the German invading forces.

their equipment and had no prospect of finding any within the city. The bombardment from German 305mm (12in) mortars was not long in coming. For many days, in the words of one German eyewitness, this bombardment formed 'the voice of Warsaw'.

Another event on 17 September helped to hasten the fate of the Poles: the Russians had begun their invasion from the east. The Bzura pocket was sealed by the *Leibstandarte*, but its duty was not over. Polish forces had withdrawn to the fortress area of Modlin, guarding the approach to Warsaw from the north; *Leibstandarte* was ordered to join 15th Corps to aid its reduction. The Polish army was by now a spectacle of

Goya-esque horror. Another firsthand *Leibstandarte* account reads:

'Our advance took us across that part of the battlefield which had been held by the so-called Pomorze army. The whole area was a scene of death and destruction. The bloated bodies of men and animals blackening under the hot sun, smashed carts, burnt-out vehicles and those most tragic victims of war, the wounded horses, waiting for the mercy shot. Everywhere there was evidence of a beaten army covering the ground ...'

Such survivors as there were huddled into the garrison forts of Modlin, which their General Thomme was soon to yield, adding 31,000 to the tally of Polish prisoners of war. The forts were pulverised by German artillery. On 25 September, the men of the *Leibstandarte* were able, in good visibility, to witness the dive-bombers of 4 Air Fleet finish the work. Two days later, Polish forces contacted General Blaskowitz and the surrender of Warsaw was signed at 1315 hours the next day. About 2000 soldiers and 10,000 civilians had perished in the siege.

Dietrich's command had, for the most part, been within orthodox military parameters. There were exceptions. Most notable among these was the arrest of Hermann Müller-John, the *Leibstandarte* band's director of music, who had rounded up a number of Polish Jews and had them shot by members of his band without any judicial investigation. His army superiors brought a charge against him, but the intervention of Hitler resulted in an amnesty a year later. This expunged from the record all other atrocities

Below: A member of the *Leibstandarte* stands guard on a Prague street. The *Leibstandarte* were sent to Czechoslovakia after their success in Poland to recuperate and replenish their losses.

known to have been committed during the Polish campaign. At the war's end, and fearing postwar reprisals, Müller-John committed suicide, along with various members of his family.

SUCCESSFUL DEBUT

As for the Polish campaign as a whole, it was widely felt that the *Leibstandarte*, its components mere battlefield fledglings, had conducted itself creditably. But criticism from the Wehrmacht would not go away. There were snide references to 'ornamental policemen', but these were muted since it was realised that Hitler would almost certainly turn a deaf ear to to any censure. There was also the realisation that any criticism of the elite guard would do the originator's career no good.

Hitler, as was always the case, had taken a close personal interest in how the SS-VT, and the *Leibstandarte* in particular, had fared. According to Otto Dietrich

Above: Frontline SS troops during mopping-up operations in Poland. *Einsatzgruppen* (SS Special Action Groups) followed the German troops into Poland, tasked with murdering national leaders and rounding up Jews.

(no relation to Sepp), Press Chief of the Reich and State Secretary to the Propaganda Ministry, during the Polish campaign, the Führer had marked on a large map the terse notation 'Sepp', which served as a marker on the progress of *Leibstandarte*.

Hitler's mood altered drastically, though, when he learnt the extent of the *Leibstandarte* casualties: 108 killed, 292 wounded, 14 lightly wounded, 3 missing and 15 accidental deaths. This was unacceptable, as he made plain at a meeting in his headquarters train

at Gross, Pomerania. According to Walther Warlimont, one of Hitler's most trusted officers, Dietrich, refusing to be cowed, had protested vigorously that the Wehrmacht support his men had the right to expect had seldom been forthcoming. Indeed, the Wehrmacht had been happy enough to throw them into battle under the most disadvantageous circumstances. General Walther von Brauchitsch, the Wehrmacht Commander in Chief, riposted that the *Leibstandarte* was untrained for battle and had no knowledge of strategy. Then had delivered the final sneer: 'They had to pay the price for being policemen dressed up in army uniforms.'

According to Warlimont, it was now Hitler's turn to be angry. He 'thumped the map table and said he

Right: Hitler on an inspection tour in Poland. The Führer was shocked by the high casualty rate suffered by all of the *Waffen-SS* units, but their success in action silenced most of their critics in the Wehrmacht.

was sick of the everlasting feud between the Army and the SS and would stand no more of it. They would either learn to work together or there would be wide plans for alteration to command.' Much to the disappointment of Dietrich and his men, there was to be no immediate return to Berlin. Instead, they were to go to Czechoslovakia in order that they might relieve *SS Der Führer*. This unit was in turn sent not to Berlin, but to the West Wall, the fortifications designed to protect the Third Reich in the west.

WARM GREETING

On arrival in Prague on 4 October, the *Leibstandarte* was greeted warmly in Wenceslas Square, not only by Constantin Freiherr von Neurath, the Reich Protector of Bohemia and Moravia, but also by the ethnic Germans of Czechoslovakia. The division's duties during this time were generally light, and there followed a period of leave for its members. However, as its leader, Sepp Dietrich was a troubled man. He was plainly restless during this quiet time and made it his business to return as soon as he could to Berlin. There, in the capital, flushed with the success of the Polish campaign and his territorial gains, Hitler was already engaged in turning his attention towards the acquisition of more territory: his new goals, France and Britain.

The men of 1st Company spent the first Christmas of World War II at Bad Ems, where each *Leibstandarte* member was awarded festive rations: a Christmas cake and some tobacco, as well as a bottle of wine. Quartering followed in the Koblenz area, once again under the command of General Guderian, who was basking in the pride of having received his Knight's Cross for the exploits of his 19th Army Corps in Poland. There was vigorous retraining, much of it during a very cold winter. The belief held by Dietrich's officers that this activity presaged forthcoming action would soon be proved correct.

CHAPTER FOUR

FRANCE

With arrogant dash, the men of the *Leibstandarte* knifed their way through to the west, brushing aside the arms and firepower of the Dutch and the French defenders in their path. To many observers, their successes seemed to prove them invincible.

Flushed with the success of victory in Poland, Hitler hoped that his next moves would come as cheaply. Therefore, at dawn on the fine spring day of 10 May 1940, the German war machine turned on the west.

For the armed SS, this was to prove a significant milestone, as was the gain this same year of the title *Waffen-SS*. For the first time, these troops would be fighting in divisional formations under the command of their own officers – although the *Leibstandarte*, by virtue of its enhanced state in the eyes of its Führer, was groomed to operate as a fully independent, motorised regiment.

At first, the precise role intended for Dietrich's men was wrapped in mystery. Hitler had visited the regiment when it was in winter quarters the previous December and had been vague about his intentions. Beyond receiving the hint that they would soon be fighting in regions where their fathers' blood had been shed, Dietrich's men learnt nothing. They had to wait until February before things became clearer: they were then located to 18th Army, which was part

Left: These fresh-faced soldiers of the *Leibstandarte* in France have been recently blooded and are already showing the strain of their rapid advance after a string of easy victories over their opponents.

of Army Group B under General Fedor von Bock. The task of General Frederick Zickwolff's 227th Infantry Division, commanding *Leibstandarte*, was to break through the Dutch frontier and, on receiving the code word 'Danzig', to capture intact the river and road bridges of the axis of advance to the Ijssel River.

FIRST STRIKE

SS-Hauptsturmführer Kurt Meyer (later to be dubbed 'Panzer' Meyer by his fellows) later recalled how a single battle group of *Leibstandarte* was positioned on the frontier bridge near the Dutch border town of De Poppe. The assault squad, overpowering the Dutch guards, cut the fuses to the bridge demolition charges and cast aside the road barrier for the waiting columns of SS vehicles. The opposition faced by the squad consisted of a rundown army fitted out with hopelessly obsolescent weapons and equipment. The most serious weakness lay in the Dutch army's ineffective anti-tank and anti-aircraft. Its main hope was to offer strong defence, to delay the progress of the enemy for as long as possible. By noon, however, the *Leibstandarte* had advanced some 80km (50 miles) over excellently maintained roads, the speed of its progress helped by the flights overhead of Junkers 52, heavily loaded with airborne troops. On reaching Bornerbroek, the *Leibstandarte* found that the key

bridge of the canal had been blown. There was no time for the SS pioneers to construct even the flimsiest of bridges; a nearby farm was pillaged and barn doors secured to do duty as rafts. The SS crossed the canal under a hail of Dutch fire.

The next objective was Zwolle, the provincial capital of Overijssel, which was reached at 1400 hours. Here things did not go so well for the Germans, in this instance for 227th Infantry Division, under whose command the *Leibstandarte* had been placed. The Dutch had foreseen a parachute drop and blown the bridges of the Ijssel. Although the defenders had destroyed both bridges, III Battalion of *Leibstandarte* forced a crossing to the south at Zutphen, eventually capturing the town and 200 defenders at Hoven, which was on the north–south main railway line.

Above: The German invasion of Holland began with the landing of paratroops from Junkers Ju 52 aircraft. The other aircraft in the picture is a Dutch fighter. The *Leibstandarte* were tasked with the capture of Zwolle.

Shortly before midday, dazed troops and frightened civilians in Zwolle greeted the advance guard of fully motorised units, this time providing yet another potent example of how the West, with its paucity of general defences, had badly underestimated the speed with which a *Blitzkrieg*, or lightning war, could be undertaken.

For the *Leibstandarte*, there was a further distinction: *SS-Obersturmführer* Hugo Krass became the first man in the campaign to win the Iron Cross First Class for his role in the crossing of the Ijssel and subsequent penetration of more than 64km (40 miles) into enemy territory. Krass, son of a schoolteacher from the Ruhr, was already the holder of the Iron Cross, Second Class, won during the Polish campaign The destruction of the Ijssel bridges, however, halted the lightning advance of Dietrich's men and the *Leibstandarte* was then withdrawn. Its next assignment was with the 9th Panzer Division and the *SS-Verfügungsdivision* in the key drive towards Rotterdam.

A significant threat was presented by the thrust of France's 7th Army, under General Henri Giraud, up through Belgium. *Verfügungsdivision* and 9th Panzer moved to relieve the *Fallschirmjäger* (paratroops), who had captured the mile-long Maas bridge at Moerdijk lying on the northern route to the key prize of Rotterdam. Giraud's forces, meanwhile, were suffering from lack of air support, armour and anti-tank and anti-aircraft guns, and were pushed back to Breda. Rotterdam obstinately stood fast; German airborne troops held the bridges, but could not cross them.

ULTIMATUM

Hitler's patience was wearing thin, as was indicated by the release of Directive No. 11 which stated: 'The power of resistance of the Dutch Army has proved to be stronger than was anticipated. Political as well as military considerations require that the resistance be broken speedily.' An ultimatum was issued: either the defenders of Rotterdam surrendered immediately or the city would suffer a massive air attack. Although the surrender was eventually forthcoming, it was not before the German bombers had been launched in an action which caused the destruction of Rotterdam. The Germans later claimed that this was an accident; at their respective trials after the war, both Hermann Göring and Albert Kesselring of the *Luftwaffe* denied that they had known of the surrender negotiations when the bombers were dispatched.

The campaign in the Netherlands was in its closing stages; for the *Leibstandarte*, any fast advance, for the moment at least, was pointless. The remit was to pass through or around Rotterdam, relieve airborne units and eventually make for The Hague. A seemingly leisurely move such as this held little appeal for either Dietrich or his men. It was at this time that an incident occurred which did the *Leibstandarte* no good whatsoever.

While German and Dutch troops inside Dutch military headquarters were busy conferring on surrender terms, they heard a massive roar of tanks and trucks hastening through the rubble. Possibly unaware of the surrender, the *Leibstandarte* confronted Dutch troops and opened fire. General Kurt Student, Commander of 7th Air Division, ran to the windows of the headquarters building to see what was happening and was clipped by a stray bullet, which severely wounded him. Dietrich and his men, not in the least repentant, later denied that any of them had fired a shot, arguing that they could not have been part of any advance involving tanks, since they did not possess armour. The blame, they insisted, must lie with 9th Panzer Division.

The truth about the *Leibstandarte*'s involvement – or lack of it – was not resolved. However, the incident did reveal that the army's reservations had been justified; predictably, it was used as a pretext for branding the *Leibstandarte* as an ill-disciplined, trigger-happy outfit. It was argued that storming through Rotterdam had been irresponsible, since it had exposed men to needless danger, particularly as, at around the time of Student's wounding, the Dutch commander in chief, General H. G. Winklemann, had been ordering all Dutch forces to capitulate. This was by no means the last criticism of *Leibstandarte*; however, for the moment, the whys and wherefores had to be swept aside amid the rushing tide of war.

First, there was to be a brief interlude before the thrust into France. In a move designed to further the humiliation of the defeated Dutch, the *Leibstandarte* and 9th Panzer Division were ordered to don their best uniforms and embark on a tour of triumph throughout southern Holland, so as to leave the local populace in no doubt as to who was master. The breakthrough operations in northern France could now proceed without hindrance. The

Right: Assisted by his staff, Sepp Dietrich (in white shirt) snatches the time during the campaign in the west in 1940 to conduct an impromptu interrogation of a captured Belgian officer.

right flank for the campaign in the west had been secured. The intention was to follow it with the separation of the British and French armies, and then their individual destruction.

The crisis point in France was the evacuation perimeter of Dunkirk, where British and French troops were compressed. On 24 May 1940, the *Leibstandarte*, under the command of Panzer Group *von Kleist*, assembled on the line of the Aa canal, along the southern and eastern side of the perimeter. On the afternoon of that day, a directive issued in Hitler's name ordered the attacking German forces not to cross the canal line; he had been persuaded to leave the destruction to Göring's *Luftwaffe*. By the time the order reached the troops, however, the *SS-Verfügungsdivision* was already in progress. Additionally, the *Leibstandarte* was about to launch its attack over the canal at Wattan, in accordance with an order by Guderian, to whose corps command *Leibstandarte* was responsible.

INSUBORDINATION

Subsequent events provided another example of the *Leibstandarte*'s penchant for insubordination. On this occasion, it was a calculated risk which did turn out to be justified. Guderian wrote in his memoirs:

'Early on 25 May I went to Watten to visit the *Leibstandarte* and to make sure that they were obeying the halt. When I arrived there I found the *Leibstandarte* engaged in crossing the Aa. On the far bank was Mont Watten, a height of only some 235 feet [71m], but that was enough in this flat marshland to dominate the whole surrounding countryside. On top of the hillock, among the ruins of an old castle, I found the divisional commander, Sepp Dietrich. When I asked why he was disobeying orders, he replied that the enemy on Mont Watten could "look right down the throat" of anybody on the bank of the canal. Sepp Dietrich had therefore decided on 24 May to take it on his own

initiative. The *Leibstandarte* and the Infantry Regiment GD [*Gross Deutschland*] on its left was now continuing their advance in the direction of Wormhoudt and Bergues. In view of the success they were having I approved the decision taken by the commander on the spot and made up my mind to order the 2nd Panzer Division to move up in their support.'

DIETRICH UNREPENTANT

Dietrich reasoned that he believed the Dunkirk advance would soon be resumed and declared later

Below: All *Waffen-SS* units, including the *Leibstandarte*, were issued with new camouflage smocks for the campaign in France and the Low Countries in 1940. The pattern was patented and worn exclusively by the SS.

that his sole motive had been to cover up for his Führer, who had clearly made an error in stopping the advance or had been persuaded into doing so by the *Wehrmacht* generals. Furthermore, he boasted that if Guderian had arrested him for court martial, he would have shot the latter on the spot.

The result of this calculated insubordination was the winning and consolidation of the bridgehead. Nonetheless, the town of Wormhoudt, already softened up by bombing and entrusted to the mercies of 2nd Battalion, remained stubbornly resistant, despite intelligence reports showing German troops outnumbering the British. Wormhoudt was of key importance because, if it was secured, it would block a path of retreat to the Channel coast for large numbers of Allied troops.

In a pocket nearby, men of 1st Company, including a *Leibstandarte* man named Tischatzki, fought hand-to-hand with a British major, an escaped prisoner who had taken sole refuge in an abandoned tank. The major seized Tischatzki's rifle and hit him hard with it; the latter retaliated and the major was eventually killed. The history of 1st Company recorded that Dietrich, impressed by the courage of the enemy soldier, ordered a funeral for him. A detachment from 1st Company fired a salute over the grave.

Slow progress at Wormhoudt was soon irking Dietrich. On 28 May – his 48th birthday, incidentally – Sepp decided to inspect forward command posts and determine the reason for the slow progress of 2nd Battalion. The powerful Mercedes set out at speed across the flat, open countryside for the small town of Esquelbecq, some two and a half kilometres (one and a half miles) from Wormhoudt. The area was supposedly a safe sector for the Germans, but the British, unhindered by the Germans, had been able to carry out a thorough mopping-up operation.

From an isolated farmhouse, a knot of British troops from the Gloucestershire Regiment brought Dietrich's car under machine-gun fire. Sepp and his companion, *Obersturmführer* Max Wünsche, quickly abandoned the burning vehicle to take refuge from the hail of bullets in a convenient culvert beneath the road. While shielding them from more fire, it at the same time exposed them to the flaming trail of petrol from the ignited fuel tank. The two men were saved, however, by ample supplies of wet mud, with which they were able to smear themselves. After rescue by elements of 2nd Panzer Brigade, a dishevelled and filthy Dietrich was deposited at Guderian's headquarters, the butt of considerable ribaldry from his men.

ATROCITY

The struggle to reach Wormhoudt itself continued meanwhile, with success eventually achieved by 2nd Battalion under its new senior company commander, Wilhelm Mohnke. A number of prisoners were captured during the course of the day. Lucas and Cooper state that Dietrich demonstrated an old-fashioned

Above: **Joachim Peiper, described as one of the most dashing officers of the war and the doyen of the *Waffen-SS*, is shown examining a roll of film during the French campaign, when he held the rank of *Hauptsturmführer* (captain).**

courtesy towards Allied prisoners, on one occasion entertaining captured British officers after the battle of Esquelbecq and presenting them with armbands and flashes as souvenirs. This was far from being the experience of all prisoners. The Royal Warwickshire Regimental History records:

'A batch of 80–90 men (made up of the 2nd Battalion, the 4th Cheshire, and some artillerymen from a passing convoy) were murdered by the SS in a barn on the outskirts of Wormhoudt. Of the Battalion prisoners, there seem to have been about 50 men from D company (together with Captain Lynne-Allen, the only officer in the group) and

some from A Company. They were double marched to the barn, and thrust at with bayonets on the way. Captain Lynn-Allen immediately protested. He was answered with taunts and several hand grenades were thrown among the crowded troops, killing and wounding many of them. Survivors were taken outside to be shot, in batches of five. After this had happened twice, those left behind refused to come out, whereupon the Germans fired indiscriminately into the barn until they judged that none [was] left alive. They judged wrongly; a few men did survive, thanks perhaps to the self-sacrifice of CSM A. Jennings and Sergeant J. Moore, who threw themselves on the top of grenades and were killed instantly by the grenades.'

One of these survivors was Private Albert Evans of the Royal Warwickshire, who was standing next to Captain Lynn-Allen when the Germans began throwing grenades. Lynn-Allen seized him, dragging him through the barn door to a clump of trees with a small stagnant pool in the centre. Here, both men took refuge, the water up to their chests.

'Suddenly without warning a German appeared on the bank of the pond just above us, showing that we must have been spotted before we gained the cover the trees. The German, who was armed with a revolver, immediately shot Captain Lynn-Allen twice. Captain Lynn-Allen's body fell forward and disappeared under the surface. The German then fired at me at a range of about three yards [three metres]. I was hit twice in the neck and, already bleeding profusely from my arm, I slumped in the water. The German no doubt thought that he had finished me off.'

The wounded Evans, leaving behind the dead who lay scattered amid guns, pouches, Bren carriers and steel helmets, managed to make his way to a house nearby, occupied by a German ambulance unit. He subsequently became a prisoner of war,

Left: Sepp Dietrich awarding Iron Crosses to men of the *Leibstandarte* following the 1940 campaign in the west. Dietrich achieved a close rapport with his men in the *Leibstandarte*. To one soldier, he was 'a father figure'.

Left: This picture from 1940 shows Dietrich's strained relationship with Himmler. The *Reichsführer-SS* deplored Dietrich's disdain for the rules, once complaining that the *Leibstandarte* was 'a complete law unto itself'.

joined by several others from the scene of the slaughter, who had given themselves up to prevent reprisals against the local population. But not all those who became prisoners survived. A further number were shot allegedly on the orders of Wilhelm Mohnke, who had been asked for 'disposal instructions'. According to the recollection of *SS-Rottenführer* Carl Kummert, who was under interrogation after the war, Mohnke's reply was that 'they had to be shot'.

MASSACRE REVEALED

The departure of the killers and the race of the *Leibstandarte* towards Paris meant that the survivors, including Private Evans, were picked up later as prisoners of war. They were able to return to Britain in a prisoner exchange in October 1943 and it was from them that the details of the massacre were first learnt. In 1941, the bodies, which had been buried hastily, were taken up by local labourers under German supervision and re-interred in Esquelbecq, Wormhoudt and elsewhere. Today, many of the graves carry the words 'buried nearby' because the SS had removed identity discs and precise identification of bodies was not always possible.

After the end of hostilities, war crimes investigators received depositions on 'the murder of 80 or 90 British prisoners of war by members of the German Armed Forces at Wormhoudt (France) on 28 May 1940'. Several German witnesses whose testimony could have proved of value had long since died – killed on the Russian front – and none of the British survivors was able positively to identify any of the men who did survive as being involved.

In 1973, Leslie Aitken, who was chaplain to the Dunkirk Veterans Association and had carried out widespread research for a book, showed pictures of two SS officers said to have been at the scene of the killings to one survivor, who picked out Dietrich. Under interrogation in the aftermath of the war, however, Dietrich had kept repeating, 'I know nothing of any shootings. I spent the day in a ditch' – the latter a reference to the assault on Wünsche and himself related above. That he remained unaware of the killings defies belief; nevertheless, it does throw an interesting light on the clannish qualities of the elite *Leibstandarte* that silence was maintained.

Attention was focused on Wilhelm Mohnke, but he remained a prisoner of the Russians until the mid-1950s. In preparing his biography of Dietrich, Charles Messenger attempted to contact Mohnke, then living in Hamburg, to obtain details, but without success. Messenger wrote: 'It was all bound up in the SS oath "my oath is my loyalty" which meant loyalty not just to state but also to fellow SS men, and this included not informing on them.'

For the *Leibstandarte*, attention now shifted away from Dunkirk and was focused on the motorised advance deep into France. For that, there was an urgent need for reinforcements, since SS casualties had been high, numbering some 3400 men, as their motorised formations had spread ahead aggressively and with total disregard for loss of life. The training schools of the Reich mustered fresh forces, which now sped eagerly to fight alongside their fellow SS comrades.

They were needed, since French resistance still had a good deal of kick in it. Attached with the SS-VT to von Kleist's Panzer Group, the *Leibstandarte* initial-

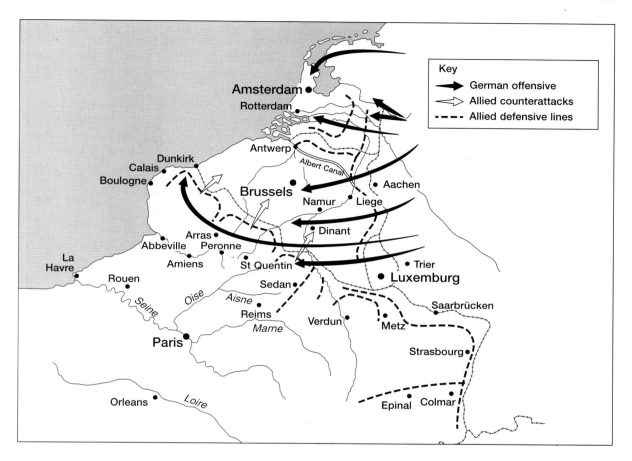

Key
- → German offensive
- ⇨ Allied counterattacks
- --- Allied defensive lines

ly made good progress across the Somme, but the degree of resistance led to it being switched to the area of Laon and on south to Chateau-Thierry, north-east of Paris. Chateau-Thierry fell to *Leibstandarte*'s 1st Battalion and the race to the Marne, which was reached on 12 June, was under way. On that date, the *Leibstandarte* established a bridgehead across the river. Two days later, Paris fell and Dietrich's men, at brief rest in the village of Etrepilly, exuberantly rang the bells of the local church.

CELEBRATION

There was indeed much cause for celebration, particularly as there was virtually no resistance as, under the command of 9th Panzer Division, the *Leibstandarte* advanced across the Seine in the fore-

Above: A map showing the German invasion of the Low Countries and the subsequent surrounding of the British Expeditionary Force at Dunkirk, from where it was evacuated. The campaign was a great success for Hitler.

front of Panzer Group *von Kleist*. At Clermond-Ferrand, 2nd Battalion paused only to seize as booty 242 aircraft and eight tanks. For Dietrich came the prize of the command of XVI Corps, which was required to take the French Army of the Alps in the rear as aid for the Italians who had invaded the French Riviera.

It was a different story on the outskirts of St Etienne, southwest of Lyons, which the *Leibstandarte* captured after it had been taken out of the line for a two-day rest. Here the attacking force was faced with a bizarre sight: the French held out for a while with some vintage World War I tanks which gave a good account of themselves.

The battle honours for the Germans were considerable. During the advance and under the orders of von Kleist, the *Leibstandarte* had made for the River Allier near Moulins, well to the north-west of Lyon. It had been an operation that provided a classic example of the battle conditions under which the *Leibstandarte* was shown at its most effective. At one of the bridges, SS infantry had found itself temporarily at a disadvantage: manpower for removing a barricade was thin on the ground. A motorcycle point detachment was pressed into action. At its head was *SS-Obersturmführer* Knittel, who rushed the defences in a head-on cycle assault, shattering the barricade. All this preceded a lightning-fast drive for Vichy, the roads leading to which were choked with French troops, with the result that the *Leibstandarte* had problems linking up with other German troops who had taken the spa town.

ARMISTICE

The French signed armistice terms on 22 June; three days later, von Bock informed Dietrich that hostilities were at an end. The cost to *Leibstandarte* during the entire campaign was 111 killed and 390 wounded. To the victor went the laurels: for Dietrich, this meant a Knight's Cross to add to the Iron Cross 1st and 2nd Class he had won in Poland. The citation read: '*Obergruppenführer* Sepp Dietrich through independent resolve in his sector during the gaining of the bridgehead over the Aa canal near Watten decisively influenced the speedy pursuit of operations in northern France and further – as before in Poland – has demonstrated personal bravery and close comradeliness with panzer and motorised formation headquarters.' The Watten bridgehead, of course, had been the scene of Sepp's act of blatant disobedience. Whether anyone was conscious of the irony remains unknown.

Such laurels were not for resting upon, however. The *Leibstandarte* avoided the victory parade in Paris, since Hitler declined to attend it, contenting himself

Right: In recognition of their role in the campaign in the west, the *Leibstandarte* were presented with a new standard by Hitler. The standard is seen here on display in Berlin in September 1940.

with a brief 'cook's tour', including a visit to Napoleon's tomb. Instead, Dietrich's men struck out on a two-day march for Metz to undergo vigorous retraining and refitting. They were briefly involved in preparations for a proposed (and later aborted) amphibious invasion of England, but this was a sideshow. On 28 July, the *Leibstandarte* received the news that it was to be expanded to brigade strength. This entailed three new rifle battalions, one heavy battalion, one artillery regiment and a reconnaissance regiment. In August, Himmler carried out a review of Hitler's Guards and attended the presentation of a new standard.

The Army refused to yield in its antagonism to the SS troops, obstructing any efforts by Himmler and his acolytes to poach further manpower. Himmler could see no way in which this stance could be reversed. He deplored: 'There is the complaint from the *Wehrmacht* that we have heard ever since 1933. Every SS man is a potential NCO but it is a pity that their commanders are so bad. After the war in Poland they said that the SS had huge casualties because they were not trained for the job. Now that we have very few losses they suppose that we have not fought.' Hitler was careful to placate the *Wehrmacht*: 'Within the framework of these armies fought the valiant divisions and regiments of the *Waffen-SS*. As a result of this war the German Armoured Corps has inscribed for itself a place in the history of the world; the men of the *Waffen-SS* have a share in this honour.' Dietric fuelled the rivalry still further with a deliberately provocative announcement: 'I, as your Regimental Commander, am proud of you and grateful that I have been allowed to lead this Regiment, the only one in the German Army with the Führer's name.'

By the start of 1941, the *Leibstandarte*'s reorganisation was complete. It was not until March, however, that the regiment left Metz and headed eastwards.

CHAPTER FIVE

THE EAST

The Greek campaign saw the last of the easy pickings for 'Hitler's own'. The tidal wave that was the German advance lost momentum in Russia, breaking against the Moscow defences. In the south, the *Leibstandarte* would experience the full impact of the Russian winter.

In the war's first 13 months, Adolf Hitler held all the cards, with a programme of conquest which had been achieved on schedule. Then, on 28 October 1940, Benito Mussolini sent the armies of Fascist Italy into Greece. This action represented one of those mood swings which were to become characteristic of Il Duce. A mere three weeks before, Mussolini had ordered mass mobilisation and Hitler had sought vainly to talk his Axis partner out of so potentially disastrous an adventure.

In the face of the invasion, the Greeks mobilised speedily and had at their disposal 15 infantry divisions, a cavalry division and four infantry brigades. The Italians mustered motorised *Bersaglieri* (elite riflemen), who poured into Greece. Within a matter of days, the Greek 9th Division counterattacked from the Macedonian mountains, led by the Greek General Alexandros Papagos's forces of around 150,000 men. A Greek *Evzone* force, made up of crack infantrymen who also served as the royal guard, trapped the Italian *Juliana* Alpine Division within gorges in the northern Pindus mountains and cut off

Left: The plains of Russia in the summer of 1941. A *Leibstandarte* anti-tank gunner looks skywards during the opening phases of Operation Barbarossa. He has goggles on his helmet to protect his eyes against the dust.

an entire Italian column. A breakout was impossible and the cost to the Duce's forces was 13,000 lives. By as early as 3 November, the Greeks were firmly on the offensive, with their troops counterattacking at points near Klissoura, Ioannina and further north at Konitsa and Kastoria. The Italians were forced back into Albania and, by mid-January, the Greeks were masters of a quarter of the country.

MUSSOLINI'S JEALOUSY

An explanation for Mussolini's all-too-conspicuous misjudgment could be traced back to Il Duce's meeting with his foreign minister, Count Galeazzo Ciano, on 12 October. The Italian dictator had complained bitterly that Hitler had stolen his thunder with the occupation of the Romanian oilfields; this act had dented Italian pride, as Mussolini had always believed the oilfields were within his sphere of influence. Il Duce fulminated: 'Hitler always faces me with a *fait accompli*. This time I am going to pay him back in his own coin. He will find out from the papers that I have occupied Greece. In this way the equilibrium will be re-established.'

Plainly, there was a threat to the Axis position in the Balkans; Hitler was faced with an unpredictable military situation on his southern flank. On 12 November, the Führer issued Directive No. 18, an

Above: In 1941 Hitler was diverted from his plans for the Soviet Union by Italy's problems in the Balkans. Here Dietrich is shown trying to clear a path for the *Leibstandarte* through a crowd of Yugoslav refugees.

order for the Army to prepare plans for the German attack on Greece, to be known as Operation Marita. Two happenings threw the original plans out of gear. The intention to seize only the Greek mainland north of the Aegean Sea was rendered inadequate because of the landing of British troops in Greece early in March. Additionally, a further decision to occupy the entire peninsula and the island of Crete was taken following the launching of Marita. Then came the second unforeseen event. Yugoslavia, along with Bulgaria, had been a signatory to the Tripartite Pact, signed by Italy, Germany and Japan, giving Hitler, as he thought, a useful ally. A military revolt in Belgrade, however, overthrew the Regency and established a new government with an anti-German

stance. The way to the Greek border was blocked. Hitler prepared Operation *Strafe* (Punishment) to coincide with Marita.

MOVE TO BULGARIA

The *Leibstandarte* was moved from Alsace via Campalung in Romania, and from there to Bulgaria, whence 12th Army was to strike towards Skoplje in southern Yugoslavia. By 7 April, the SS, under the command of XL Corps, had followed 9th Panzer in its drive from the border town of Kustendil.

The XL Corps assault had been planned in two columns. In the north, 9th Panzer and *Leibstandarte* forced the Kriva Pass and captured Skoplje, which lay some 95km (60 miles) inside Yugoslavia. Here, the *Leibstandarte* was to smart from a Yugoslav air attack which seriously injured Wilhelm Mohnke, the commander of 2nd Battalion, and one of the battery commanders. The southern arm, consisting of 73rd Infantry Division, then captured the strategically

Above: A *Leibstandarte* machine gun team move though one of the passes during the attack on Greece. Although the Greek and Allied defenders fought bravely, the German *Blitzkrieg* was victorious again.

important town of Prilep before advancing south to Bitola, which was secured after house-to-house fighting. A reconnaissance battalion, under the command of Kurt 'Panzer' Meyer, was split. One half probed the Monastir Gap, known as the gateway to Greece, while the other turned west to meet the Italians on the Albanian border. At the entrance to the Klidi Pass, on the border with Greece, the Germans faced Australian, New Zealand and British troops under Lieutenant General Sir Henry Maitland Wilson, who had been sent to help in Greece's defence.

On the morning of 10 April, the Klidi Pass, with it numerous heights, was attacked by *Sturmbannführer* Fritz Witt, who faced considerable opposition from the 6th Australian Division. For many of the SS men,

this was their first sighting of Imperial troops, whom one *Leibstandarte* participant dismissed condescendingly as 'mercenaries'. He also commented that the Australians 'do not seem to be as well disciplined as the English nor do they wear their uniform as a soldier should'. The prize of capturing Height 997 after hand-to-hand fighting went to *Obersturmführer* Gert Pleiss, along with the Knight's Cross. After three days of conflict, the cost to the *Leibstandarte* was 37 killed, 98 wounded and two missing. By way of compensation, however, some weaponry had been captured and the road to Greece lay open.

The hour belonged not to Witt, but to the former policeman and labourer's son *SS-Sturmbannführer* Kurt 'Panzer' Meyer, who was ordered to advance through the Klissoura Pass to Lake Kastoria, in order to strike at the Greek division protecting the British left flank. In his memoirs, *Grenadiere*, Meyer, another recipient of the Knight's Cross, related how he and a small group inched along the road through the pass, while two of his companies scaled the cliffs to take the defenders in the flank. The main onslaught was conducted amid the smoke, dirt and confusion which followed the release by the Greeks of their main demolition charges.

DESPERATE MEASURES

'We glue ourselves behind rocks and dare not move. A feeling of nausea tightens my throat. I yell to (*Untersturmführer*) Emil Wawrzinek to get the attack moving. But the good Emil just looks at me as if he has doubts about my sanity. Machine-gun fire smacks against the rocks in front of us … How can I get

Below: Despite their pith helmets, these men of the *Leibstandarte* are not in Africa but Greece, during the German invasion. Pith helmets allowed far more of a soldier's body heat to escape than the regular issue steel.

Wawrzinek to take that first leap? In my distress, I feel the smooth roundness of an egg hand grenade in my hand. I shout at the group. Everybody looks thunderstruck at me as I brandish the hand grenade, pull the pin, and roll it precisely behind the last man. Never again did I witness such a concerted leap forward as at that second. As if bitten by tarantulas, we dive around the rock spur and into a fresh crater. The spell is broken. The hand grenade has cured our lameness. We grin at each other, and head forward towards the next cover.'

Kastoria was taken by Meyer's battalion, with 11,000 prisoners captured. By 20 April, the SS unit had taken the Mesovan Pass, with the result that the Greek units on the west side of the Pindus mountains were isolated. The *Leibstandarte* had blocked the line of withdrawal. The Greek leaders were compelled to sue for an armistice. On the morning of 20 April

Above: Flushed with their recent triumph in northern Greece, members of the *Leibstandarte* load up prior to a perilous ferrying across the Gulf of Corinth in preparation for an unstoppable sweep south.

1941, at the Katara Pass (which served as the sole entrance to Epirus through the Pindus range), a Greek staff officer, part of an escort of a motorcycle and two cars, informed a German platoon leader that the entire Greek army in Epirus was prepared to surrender 16 divisions. This was followed by the arrival, to cheers from his men, of a euphoric Sepp Dietrich.

Writer James Weingartner records that the instrument of surrender drafted by Dietrich and the Greek General Tsolakoglou was 'chivalrous, even anachronistic in the context of World War II. Officers were

allowed to retain their weapons and enlisted men, after having surrendered their arms, were permitted to retire to their homes.' On 20 April, Hitler's 52nd birthday, the two principals returned to the pass for the actual signing, which took place under both national flags.

SWASTIKA OVER THE ACROPOLIS

British and Imperial forces now represented the sole opposition. On 24 April, the pursuit across the Pindus mountains by the *Leibstandarte* began, but the Allied forces had evacuated. In Athens, the swastika flew over the Acropolis. Dietrich's men now progressed south through the Peleponnese to the embarkation ports, having been ferried across the Gulf of Corinth after taking the port of Patros. The brigade was permitted

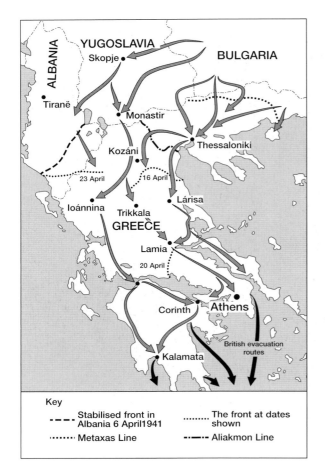

Key

– – – Stabilised front in Albania 6 April 1941	········ The front at dates shown
·········· Metaxas Line	–··–··– Aliakmon Line

Above: The attack on Greece. The *Leibstandarte* seized the Monastir Pass before moving south, brushing aside the Greek and Allied opposition. The cost of the campaign for the *Leibstandarte* was only 93 killed.

to participate in the victory parade in Athens and there had been a few days enjoyment of the Greek sunshine. Leave was short-lived, however, along with any time to count the cost of the campaign. That, as revealed in the surviving records of the *Reichsführer-SS*, had been a loss to the *Leibstandarte* of 93 killed, 225 wounded and three missing. The *Leibstandarte* was now destined to be sent to Prague to be refitted for the invasion of the Soviet Union, which had been delayed by events in the Balkans.

In the time leading up to the Soviet campaign, significant changes took place in the policy of *Waffen-SS* recruitment. The SS now began to draw on *Volksdeutsche* – those of German ancestry living outside Germany's frontier – and also upon non-German 'Nordics' for its manpower. It was not a development which pleased the narrow ideological straitjacket worn by Heinrich Himmler, but *Wehrmacht* authority was dictating that only slim numbers of Reich Germans should be permitted to join the distrusted *Waffen-SS*. The lack of recruits was thus a serious issue and one which the input of *Volksdeutsche* could help to remedy.

The *Leibstandarte*, however, was to prove an exception to this widening net because of its unique elite character; it alone was to be preserved by Himmler as a purely German unit. Such racial correctness may have been irreproachable, but it would hardly solve the manpower problem. *Leibstandarte* was still around only brigade strength and could command little more than half the strength of *Das Reich*, *Totenkopf* and the newly formed *Wiking*. As a result of this, during the course of a refit, *Leibstandarte* was given an additional motorised infantry battalion and officially designated SS Division *Leibstandarte Adolf Hitler*. These reorganisations inevitably spelt delay, which meant that the newly designated division was not destined to cross the Soviet frontier until the later date of 1 July 1941.

Previously, German radio listeners had awoken on the morning of 22 June to the voice of Propaganda Minister Joseph Goebbels, who had intoned the Führer's proclamation: 'Weighed down with heavy cares, condemned to months of silence, I can at last speak freely, German people! At this moment, a march is taking place that, for its extent, compares with the greatest that the world has ever seen. I have decided again today to place the state and future of the Reich and our people in the hands of our soldiers. May God aid us, especially in this fight!'

SURPRISE ATTACK

Four hours before Goebbels' broadcast had taken place, Russian border frontier guards had stared in

Above: Sepp Dietrich conducts a ceremony with the *Leibstandarte* at the site of the ancient Olympic Games in Greece. The SS and Himmler in particular were keen to link their activities with ancient traditions and practices.

disbelief at a dawn sky fractured with the brilliant flashes from German guns. Punch drunk and fumbling with their tunic buttons, the guards stumbled from their barracks, gasping and choking through the smoke. To the sound and sight of the guns was then added the squeal and the clatter and the thud of tanks. Hitler's units were crossing a 3200-km (2000-mile) front in the first act of Directive No. 21, code-named Operation Barbarossa.

The delayed role of the *Leibstandarte* needs to be considered in the context of that of the other *Waffen-SS* divisions. These were ultimately responsi-

ble to three field marshals. The *Leibstandarte* and *Wiking* divisions were part of Army Group South, commanded by Gerd von Rundstedt, who had been promoted after the fall of France. The same promotion had been afforded to Wilhelm Ritter von Leeb, whose Army Group North included the *Totenkopf* and *Polizei* divisions. Army Group Centre, under Fedor von Bock, who had also become a field marshal the previous year, included *Das Reich* (formerly the *SS-VT* Division). But, for the *Waffen-SS*, this was initially to be a strictly subsidiary role within Operation Barbarossa; its total strength amounted to only 160,405 men. The strength of the *Leibstandarte* itself was 10,796 men. The *Waffen-SS* soldiers had to come to terms with a front which could stretch from the woods and snow of northern Finland, through the wide steppe land of Central

Russia, and reach out to the high mountains of the subtropical Caucasus.

HUGE UNDERTAKING

The logistics alone were almost unfathomable: apart from the movement of men, there was overall a call for 600,000 vehicles, 750,000 horses, more than 7000 pieces of artillery and 3000 tanks. All these were to be pitted against an enemy that was an almost wholly unknown factor and in terrain that bore no relation to that of the west. Under a two-hour fall of rain, the primitive, pitted roads of the east could be reduced to swamps which held entire tank columns in a sticky embrace. The Germans based their concept of the Soviet armed forces on the poor showing of the Red Army in combat against the Finns in the winter of 1938–40. This proved a cardinal error, as one participant, *SS-Obergruppenführer* Max Simon, pointed out:

'The Russian infantryman ... always defended himself to the last gasp ... even crews in burnt-out tanks kept up fire for as long as their was breath in their bodies ... Wounded or unconscious men reached for their weapons as soon as they regained consciousness ... A Russian patrol driven off from our line would leave behind a small detachment which would remain concealed for days and be gradually reinforced until at a specified time and place a large body of enemy troops would emerge ... No water or swamp was too deep and no forest too thick for them to find a way through.'

The 46 divisions which made up von Rundstedt's Army Group South – composed of 6th, 11th and 17th Armies and bolstered by 1st Panzer Group of General Edwald von Kleist – closed up the Polish border with the Soviet Union. Army Group South was to cut off

Below: The *Leibstandarte*'s final rehearsal for Operation Barbarossa, due for 22 June 1941, watched by Field Marshal Gerd von Rundstedt (left) commander of Army Group South and Sepp Dietrich (centre).

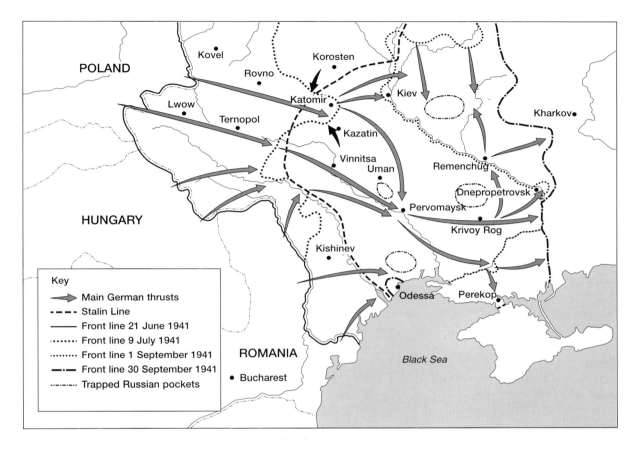

Key

→ Main German thrusts
- - - Stalin Line
—— Front line 21 June 1941
······· Front line 9 July 1941
········· Front line 1 September 1941
—·— Front line 30 September 1941
—··—·· Trapped Russian pockets

and destroy the Russian forces west of the River Dniepr, with the 1st Panzer Group on the left flank slicing through below Kovel, which lay to the east of Lublin. This was to be followed by a vast pincer embrace. Such a summary can take no account of the distances involved. Army Group South held a line from the southern end of the Pripet Marshes to the Black Sea and its first mammoth bound was from the frontier to the Dniepr, a distance of 480km (300 miles). The main prize was to be Rostov and that lay a further 1120km (700 miles) beyond.

The *Leibstandarte* had been posted to the Lublin area, under the command of Colonel-General Edwald von Kleist, as one of three motorised divisions. The division made for Ostorwiecz, with the destination of the Vistula and, ultimately, the wide steppes of Galicia, reaching the western Ukraine on

Above: A map showing the progress of Army Group South (of which the *Leibstandarte* was a part) during Operation Barbarossa, the invasion of the Soviet Union. Large numbers of Soviet prisoners were taken by the Germans.

30 June. It had been seen on its way with a flurry via a radio feature called 'The SS at War' orchestrated by Goebbels' Propaganda Ministry. Broadcasts such as this were regularly monitored by the British, who had picked up coverage of a parade of *Leibstandarte*'s 1st Battalion, the commentary of which has survived in part:

'These are the men of the *Leibstandarte*, soldiers of the Führer, trained and educated in the spirit of the SS during the years of peace; seasoned and proven in the best soldierly tradition on all the battlefields of this war. The *Leibstandarte* and the other divisions of the *Waffen-SS* form part of the great structure of the armed forces. They are fighting at the front to safeguard the honour, greatness and freedom of the Reich against the external enemy. They have come from the ranks of the SS, the ranks of those men whose task it was and still is to protect the Führer and safeguard the Reich internally. Only the best German and Germanic men are worthy of or equal to this lofty task. The aim of the SS Head Office, in its capacity as Chapter of the Order, is the political soldier of the Germanic Order. Therefore the basic law of the SS is the law of race and selection.'

SHOCK FOR THE SS

Over the next two weeks, the division was to come up against an enemy whose forces seemed indifferent to their fate. On one occasion, it faced infantry who fired from unprotected open trucks or leapt over the sides of their vehicles and charged the Germans on foot. An additional shock was the sudden experience of something hitherto unknown to the SS, the position of being stuck fast and involved in a series of defensive actions. The 73rd Panzer Division faced just this situation under heavy assault on the Kiev road. *Leibstandarte* had to lend its strength, with the consequent loss of some 683 killed and wounded. At this stage of the campaign, repulsing the attacks was comparatively easy.

The Russians strove desperately to stem the German tide around the city of Lvov, which they lost only after eight days of bitter fighting which had included a tank battle with *Wiking*. The Soviet South-West Front (Army Group) Commander, General Mikhail Kirponos, ordered his troops to pull back to the 'Stalin Line', a source of defences combining concrete, field works and natural obstacles which lay behind the River Sluch. This they did while delivering fierce counterattacks against the forces of von Kleist. But the line, they found, consisted largely of pill-boxes and anti-tank barriers which had not been strengthened since the frontier moved west. On 8 July, von Kleist was able to penetrate it; the 13th Panzer Division pressed on to secure Zhitomir, the next prize and the last major town before Kiev.

By now thinly stretched and increasingly vulnerable to air assaults, *Leibstandarte* followed in the wake of 13th Panzer to repulse counterattacks. No respite was expected, however, and nor was any granted. Army Group South was in a position to seize Kiev, a tempting prize, but this goal gave von Rundstedt pause. He saw that the railway network, vital for the deployment of Soviet troops, converged at another major junction. That junction was at Uman, a valuable communications centre, which had links south to the Crimea. Von Rundstedt reasoned that it might be better to bypass Kiev for the moment and turn south to Uman.

As it turned out, events overtook any option. The Soviet Marshal Semyon Budenny, with his 11th and 17th Armies and a force of Romanians, was advancing towards Odessa on the Black Sea. A section of Budenny's forces had been ordered to hold Odessa and the rest to concentrate on Uman. Von Kleist's tanks surged forwards through heavy rain. Once again, a Soviet counterattack consisted largely of trucks crammed with infantry driving flat out at German tanks. It proved hopeless, however, as von Kleist's forces linked up with 17th Army on the River Bug, some 80km (50 miles) beyond Uman. The weather then changed and, under a fierce sun, German infantry marched across the rough terrain. After a series of battles, a circle of steel trapped and sealed the pocket; within it were 6th, 12th and part of 18th Red Army, and 100,000 prisoners for the Germans.

Counterattacks to break the German encirclement were relentless. One SS man wrote: 'We are all exhausted from lack of sleep. We seem to have been fighting without adequate sleep for weeks now ... I've lost all track of time.' Soviet breakthrough attempts were made first by armoured cars and cavalry, and then by tanks, all of whom succeeded briefly in entering the town. The pocket was sealed, however, by the rapid advance of 1st Panzer back along the line on the way to Zhitomir, where it linked up with armoured elements of a Hungarian infantry division, clamping down hard on 25 Soviet divisions. By 1 August, the Russian defences at Novo Archangelsk were breached. The Uman pocket remained sealed.

Above: A member of the *Leibstandarte* controls a crowd of distraught Polish women as their menfolk are rounded up by an *Einsatzgruppen* squad sometime before the invasion of the Soviet Union in late June 1941.

The action earned *Leibstandarte* the highest praise from the Corps Commander Major General Werner Kempf:

'Since 24/7, the *Leibstandarte SS Adolf Hitler* has taken the most glorious part in the encirclement of the enemy around Uman. Committed at the focus of the battle for the seizure of the key enemy position at Archangelsk, the *Leibstandarte SS Adolf Hitler*, with incomparable dash, took the city and the heights to the south. In the spirit of the most devoted brotherhood of arms, they intervened on their own initiative in the arduous struggle of the 16th Infantry Division

(motorised) on their left flank and routed the enemy, destroying numerous tanks.

'Today at the conclusion of the battle of annihilation around Uman, I want to recognise and express my personal thanks to the *Leibstandarte SS Adolf Hitler* for their exemplary effort and incomparable bravery. The battles around Archangelsk will be recorded indelibly and forever in the war history of the *Leibstandarte Adolf Hitler*.'

FRESH TARGETS

The success of the action at Uman meant that advance could continue and all eyes were on the lower Dniepr, with *Leibstandarte* proceeding towards the large industrial city of Kherson, northeast of Odessa on the Black Sea, which was to fall on 19 August after fierce street fighting. The advance

Right: Proudly displaying for the photographer the captured standards of Russian units they have beaten, men of the *Leibstandarte* guard dejected Soviet prisoners waiting to begin the long march to a prison camp.

brought with it scattered benefits in the vicinity of the town of Sasselje, where a good deal of the fighting was done in maize and sunflower fields. A group of Russian troops who thought that they had found a point of retreat blundered straight into the Germans and paid the price.

It was during this time that, according to an allegation made in 1948 by one of the division's surviving members, the *Leibstandarte* was responsible for one of its most grievous atrocities on the Eastern Front. Erick Kern, a journalist who had served with the *Leibstandarte* Division's 4th Battalion, alleged in a book, *Der Grosse Rausch (The Great Ecstasy)* that, at the end of one day's fighting, two companies could not be contacted and his battalion was ordered to find them. Eight kilometres (five miles) east of the village of Gejgova (or, in another account, Grejgowo), the bodies of 103 officers and men from the elusive companies were discovered hanging in a cherry orchard and, subsequently, the bodies of six others who had clearly been shot after surrendering were also found. According to Kern, orders were received from Division that all Soviet prisoners were to be shot as reprisal and that the toll was 4,000 Russians, who were to be despatched at the edge of an anti-tank ditch in batches of eight.

Histories of the *Waffen-SS* by Gerald Reitlinger and George H Stein claim that it was not orders from the division which sealed the fate of the prisoners, but rather an order from Sepp Dietrich. No documentation or reliable eyewitness testimony ever emerged, although the Soviets did take a large number of prisoners around this time. Charles Messenger, citing another source in his biography of Dietrich, quotes a claim that Dietrich did everything possible to prevent reprisals being carried out on prisoners, stating: 'We owe it to the title on our sleeves.'

At the height of the successes achieved by Army Group Centre, most notably the fall of Smolensk,

Hitler made a momentous intervention. The Führer had never shared fully the eagerness of his generals to take Moscow, dismissing the capital as a 'geographical expression', rather than the Soviet nerve centre. His attention had become focused instead on the agricultural resources and industrial yields of the Ukraine. A delay in the push towards Moscow was ordered on 23 July 1941. Colonel-General Hoth's Panzer Group was told to turn north to take Leningrad, while Guderian was to join the advance in the Ukraine to Kiev and beyond, with the aim of destroying the armies of Marshal Budenny east of the Dniepr. Only then would Moscow be the objective.

For the *Leibstandarte*, whose reconnaissance battalion remained under the command of 'Panzer' Meyer, it was to be above all a change of climate – a move to desert country, to the enveloping, reddish brown dust

of the trackless Nogai Steppe and the Perekop Isthmus. This was the gateway to the Crimea, heavily fortified by minefields and the support of an armoured train. The attention of General Erich von Manstein, the new commander of 11th Army, was to be diverted, however, by a limited Soviet counterattack against part of the 3rd Romanian Army which tore a large gap in the line, threatening isolation of his own forces. Not for the first time, Sepp Dietrich's men were required for a rescue mission. They were diverted to the Gavrilovka area near Melitopol, where they counterattacked the Soviet forces and were

Below: A *Leibstandarte* motorcyclist passes two flak guns from the unit's flak battery in the Ukraine. Note the number of fuel cans tied to the trailer – huge quantities of fuel were needed to cross the vast spaces of the Soviet Union.

instrumental in restoring the German–Romanian line. Von Kleist, in charge of the newly designated lst Panzer Army, moved south from Kiev – which was destined to fall on 19 September – and eventually achieved a link-up with von Manstein on the Sea of Azov. It was to be the culmination of six days of heavy fighting and an aggressive drive eastwards which had covered almost 400km (250 miles).

DOUBTS ARISE

For Amy Group South, the results so far in this war had been gratifying; there had been substantial gains,

Below: The members of the *Leibstandarte* shown here have been caught on camera while preparing to enter a Russian village soon after the invasion of the Soviet Union in the summer of 1941.

even if they had not been obtained cheaply. However, ever since the first encounter with the Russians, a doubt had lurked even in the minds of the most dedicated SS men. What real chance had they in this inhospitable land with its vast reaches and seemingly limitless manpower? A few million casualties would be as nothing. Into the mind of some of the older officers there floated a saying recalled from World War I: '*Viele Hunde sind der Tod des Hasen*' ('Many hounds spell death to the hare').

And then there was the Russian winter, which was not simply snow – although there was to be plenty of that. There was also the November rain, needle-sharp downpours that swept straight into the column. Bitter cold froze lubricating oil and cracked the cylinders of engines in tanks and trucks. Adequate supplies of food could not be got through, nor replacements for

boots or socks that rotted away in the filth and wet. The winter struck with particular harshness around the city of Rostov, where frostbite took its toll on lives. Dietrich himself suffered frostbite on the toes of his right foot. Dysentery was another scourge, one which made 'Panzer' Meyer its victim.

On 17 November, after assault from the north had been scrapped due to the strength of Soviet opposition, *Leibstandarte* launched its attack on Rostov from the coast. This was a vast, depressing wasteland for the SS, one of whom recorded:

'There is very little water and what there is salty. Coffee tastes of salt, the soup seems to be full of salt … but we are pleased to get even this tepid liquid because this is true desert country. Movement is visible for miles; clouds of choking, red-brown dust hang over our columns when we are moving and pinpoint our exact positions. Paradoxically, the only signs of life are the dead tree trunks of telegraph poles. Without them it would be difficult to orientate oneself … sometimes we find a melon field and gorge ourselves, but the unripe fruits have unhappy effects'

ROSTOV FALLEN

On 22 November, a statement was issued from III Corps which declared that Rostov had fallen, thereby giving to the Germans an important commercial and traffic centre 'of decisive importance for the further prosecution of the war'. It was true that III Corps had broken into the city, securing 10,000 prisoners, 159 guns, 56 tanks and two armoured trains. There had also been a sweep through to the Don. All this had been achieved, however, by men whose strength was vitiated by dysentery and battle losses. Dwindling fuel stocks meant that movement by even the healthy was impeded. With almost surgical precision, the Soviet 37th Army exploited the only too abundant weaknesses in the German lines.

For eight days, amid the biting cold of this Russian winter, those who were able battled against the Soviet forces – infantry from three divisions, buttressed by heavy armour – and a press-ganged citizen militia. Many could only lie in trenches, their heads covered with tarpaulins thick with ice. Many died there. Things were little better with troops in the south. Nevertheless, a letter from General Eberhardt von Mackensen's Corps to Himmler extolled the *Leibstandarte* for 'its discipline … cheerfulness, energy and unshakeable steadfastness in time of crisis … a real elite unit …

'I can assure you that the *Leibstandarte* enjoys an outstanding reputation not only with its superiors, but also among its Army comrades. Every division wishes it had the *Leibstandarte* as its neighbour, as much during the attack as in defence … A genuine elite formation that I am happy to have under my command and, furthermore, one that I sincerely and hopefully wish to retain …'

After the war's end, the writer James Lucas was given access to a *Leibstandarte* man's diary which painted a far less rosy (but more accurate) picture than that presented to the *Reichsführer-SS*: 'It is not possible in words to describe winter on this front. There is no main battle line, no outposts, no reserves. Just small groups of us depending upon each other to hold defended points … Here life is paralysed … you would never believe the lavatory procedures … And the food … we live on a sort of thick soup made of ground buckwheat and millet. We have to strip the fallen, theirs and ours, for warm clothing. I don't think I will ever be warm again and our tame Ivans say this is a mild winter. May God preserve us.'

The diary entry went on to describe tanks and guns that had been rendered useless because of the cold, making infantry weapons the sole means of defence. Death, when it came, was not only from enemy fire. A unit which had been driven from its positions onto an exposed steppe needed to find some form of shelter – any shelter – before men were attacked by icy winds which could slash through them like a scythe. When the Russians did come in, it was 'in masses so great as to numb the senses. They had to pick their way through the dead of the other assaults who are still unburied. We drove them all off – how easy it seems to write this – and when they had gone back across the ice the whole area to both flanks and in front of our positions was carpeted with dead. They were dead

Above: The Ukraine, August 1941. An armoured car, with its *Leibstandarte* badge prominent on its rear, supports an infantry squad engaged in clearing a town. In the early stages of the war resistance was often sporadic and light.

all right … the wounded die quickly; the blood freezes as it leaves the body and a sort of shock sets in which kills. Light wounds that heal in three days in summer kill you in winter.'

Troops fighting in this alien land, ill-equipped and outgunned, were on a hiding to nothing. The climate had nothing to offer, either. According to General Hans von Greiffenburg, Chief of Staff to 12th Army: 'The effect of climate in Russia is to make things impassable in the mud of spring and autumn, unbearable in the heat of summer and impossible in the depths of winter. Climate in Russia is a series of natural disasters.'

SOVIET CONFIDENCE

One Soviet prisoner, secured at the time, claimed that the Soviet Union would win the war, as it pos-

sessed three basic advantages. Firstly, Soviet soil and sand would clog up and therefore ruin the engines of the German vehicles and render them immobile. Secondly, Soviet partisans would sever supply lines, encouraging the High Command to withdraw front-line troops and garrison the rear areas. Thirdly, and it was this that stuck in the minds of many, in the words of the Soviet prisoner: 'When the winter comes then our war will start, now it has only been your war.'

'Panzer' Meyer wrote: 'We were already on the retreat, straggling back … across country that resembled those 1916 pictures of the Menin Road. Every now and then we turned and made a little foray against the Ruskies, and some of them killed off a few; but in less than a week we had lost hundreds of our own men and vehicles. For the first time the *Leibstandarte* had experienced a major defeat. We weren't outfought, but we were outnumbered, overwhelmed, pushed to the wall by sheer weight. And we didn't know where the replacements were coming from.'

Right: As winter began to set in, the retreating Soviet troops continued their 'scorched earth' policy, denying any shelter to the men of the *Leibstandarte* as they advanced, leaving them vulnerable to the cold.

To von Rundstedt, it was becoming increasingly clear that the sorely pressed German forces, facing a Russian counterattack, were not up to defending Rostov. It made sense to fall back to the better defended Mius line and orders to that effect were given to von Kleist. There was retaliation of such intensity from the Russians, however, that there was the risk that von Kleist would find himself cut off from the rest of Army Group South.

On hearing of this, Hitler flew into one of his rages and ordered no further retreat. Von Rundstedt stood firm, wiring the Führer: 'It is madness to attempt to hold. In the first place the troops cannot do it, and in the second place if they do not retreat they will be destroyed. I repeat that this order be rescinded or that you find someone else.' Hitler, as it turned out to his later personal regret, accepted the challenge and von Rundstedt was relieved of his command, to be replaced by Field Marshal Walter von Reichenau, who died of a stroke within months.

As far as Dietrich was concerned, the situation regarding Rostov was not without irony. Hitler had not only sacked von Rundstedt, but also branded von Kleist a coward. The Führer's next move was to take a flight to meet Dietrich and assess the situation for himself. The latter found himself actually defending the generals against Hitler's wrath.

No one could deny the contribution that *Leibstandarte* had made. Dietrich, in the short term at least, could feel satisfied with the role that his men had played. The year 1941 was rounded off handsomely with the presentation of the Oak Leaves to his Knight's Cross, given, proclaimed Hitler, as 'demonstrable recognition of my pride in your and my Regiment's achievements'. The reality, though, was stark. A number of Soviet armies had been destroyed, but the Red Army was still intact and, even more menacing to contemplate, the sources of manpower for the Soviets were seemingly limitless.

CHAPTER SIX

KURSK

In the greatest tank battle of the war, more than 6000 tanks clashed in the Kursk salient, and although *Leibstandarte* performed well, the German *Blitzkrieg* was finally beaten. By the end of the battle, the Germans had permanently lost the initiative on the Eastern Front.

The deep severity of the winter of 1941–42 had inevitably slowed down widespread military activity on the Russian front. A Soviet offensive and local breakthrough near Dnepropetrovsk, south-east of Kharkov, brought III Corps out to seal the breach; the *Leibstandarte* held the line while the German operation was executed. It was not until the thaw and the mud had cleared, and the vehicles were able to move, that Army Group South could fulfil the order to destroy the enemy in front of the Don with the eventual aim of seizing the oil-producing centres of the Caucasus.

Hitler now had a fresh preoccupation. Along with another period of refitting and reinforcement, *Leibstandarte* was plucked from the command of Army Group South in June and sent to the coast of France, where the Führer believed an Allied invasion was possible. Meanwhile, the Nazi leader had recognised that the progress of his war was dictating the need for increased manpower and a tighter, more cohesive command centre. The *Leibstandarte*'s panzer battalion was enlarged into a regiment of two tank battalions.

Left: Amid burnt-out ruins, a *Leibstandarte* motor cycle patrol await the clearance of the thaw and mud which followed the deep severity of winter. It was obvious to many that 1943 offered the last chance for a German victory.

Added muscle was provided by an early appearance of the new 60-ton tank leviathans, the Tigers. Infantry was beefed with two panzer grenadier regiments, while artillery now had four battalions. During the closing months of 1942, the *Leibstandarte* was designated SS Panzer Grenadier Division *Leibstandarte SS Adolf Hitler*. The result of all these changes was increased recruitment, but any head count was misleading since some 75 per cent of the men was deficient in training.

DIRE OUTLOOK

The re-emergence of the *Leibstandarte* on the Eastern Front at the end of December 1942 coincided with an increasingly dire outlook for the Wehrmacht, which was faced with nothing less than the collapse of the entire Southern Front. East of Kharkov, Hungarian and Italian satellite armies were in disarray. On 12 January 1943, there was a massive Soviet attack from Orel to Rostov. Then came the death ride of 6th Army at Stalingrad, with the loss of more than 200,000 men. It was a sad irony for those who, back in October 1941, had heard Hitler address the German people and proclaim: 'I declare today, and I declare it without any reservation, that the enemy in the east has been struck down and will never rise again … Behind our troops there already lies a territory twice the size of the German Reich when I came to power in 1933.'

SS Panzer Corps, commanded by General of Mountain Troops Hubert Lanz, had been assigned the task of defending Kharkov by General (later Field Marshal) Erich von Manstein, an order backed by Hitler, who had declared that at all costs the city must be held. At deployment, the *Leibstandarte* took up a defensive position along the Donetz, with *Das Reich* holding outposts east of the river. The troops were thinly spread along a front stretching some 110km (70 miles) at Chegevayev, which was on the Donetz itself. They were under the temporary command of Fritz Witt, who was standing in for an absent Dietrich, the latter having been called to conference with Hitler. Lanz's men were forced back in a swirl of snowstorms which failed to hinder the Russian advance.

Total annihilation faced 320th Infantry Division, fighting its way back to the Donetz line and saddled with 1500 wounded whose comrades were not prepared to surrender to the Russians. Once again, enter the *Leibstandarte* in a 'fire brigade' role. This time, the initiative belonged to *SS-Sturmbannführer* Jochen Peiper, who led the 3rd Battalion of 2nd SS Panzer Division. It penetrated deep into enemy territory, forming a protective screen to release the wounded and pull back to the Donetz. Unfortunately, the ice on the river was too thin to bear Peiper's armoured vehicles. He was faced with the intimidating prospect of turning back into enemy territory and finding an area where the river could safely be forded.

KHARKOV

All attention was now on Kharkov, however, which was virtually surrounded and where Hitler refused to countenance withdrawal. The packs of Soviet tanks had penetrated to the edge of the city, rendering northern, northwestern and southeastern defences useless. *SS-Obergruppenführer* Paul Hausser made a cool survey of the situation. The corps diary entry 138/43 of 14 February 1943 read in part: 'Inside Kharkov mob firing at troops and vehicles. No forces available for mopping up since everything in front

line. City, including railway, stores and ammunition dumps, effectively dynamited at Army orders. City burning. Systematic withdrawal increasingly improbable each day … Request renewed Führer decision.' The reply was predictable: 'Panzer Corps will hold to the last man.' General Lanz saw himself as his master's voice and stood firm.

Hausser was an experienced general staff officer of the old Imperial army who had retired from the *Reichswehr* with the rank of lieutenant general and who, conscious of the need for self-preservation, had later enlisted with the *Waffen-SS*. Even so, he was prepared to challenge Hitler and pressed his case, but Lanz still refused to allow withdrawal. During the night 14/15 February, the Russians had broken into the northwestern and southwestern parts of the city. Conscious that he was putting his entire career on the line, Hausser ignored both his Führer's order and the obduracy of Lanz. He mounted a break-out to the south-west between the encircling Russian armies, regrouping around Krasnograd.

The news of the withdrawal was greeted by an ecstatic Stalin: 'The mass expulsion from the Soviet Union has begun.' The newly self-proclaimed Marshal of the Soviet Union was premature in his celebration, but the abandonment of Kharkov, however temporary, *was* an indication of how Germany's fortunes in the east were changing. In a fine fury, Hitler took an aircraft to von Manstein's headquarters, demanding Hausser's dismissal, but was persuaded that no alternative to the yielding of Kharkov had been possible. Mollified, Hitler reprieved Hausser and sacked Lanz instead. Still, the Führer managed to signify his disapproval by postponing Hausser's Oak Leaves to his Knight's Cross.

Von Manstein's plan, to be implemented by Hausser, was to stand firm at Krasnograd, thus luring the pursuing Russians into a trap. Strength was improved by the arrival of the *Totenkopf* division, which had earlier linked up with the three panzer divisions of 48th Panzer Corps. The two armoured corps, one Army and one SS, as the components of 4th Panzer Army, went on to launch a concerted attack with effective air support northwards towards Pavlograd and

Losuvaya. On 25 February, 4th Panzer Army wiped out a Soviet army group led by General M.M. Popov.

This undoubtedly boosted morale, as did the trapping of Soviet forces between the defensive lines of 1st SS Panzer Grenadier Division and the two attacking divisions of the SS Panzer Corps. By 3 March, the Soviet forces had been encircled west of Bereka, which lay north of Krasnograd on a direct line to Kharkov. Three days later, the Corps had reached Valki, which lay to the north-west of the city. The aim was to thrust the Russians back across the Donetz. With that objective achieved by the advanced guard of the *Leibstandarte*, the assault on Kharkov was under way. The order came from Colonel General Hermann Hoth, as commander of 4th Panzer Army, 'to seal off

Above: Soldiers from the *Leibstandarte* relax during the summer of 1942 in the Ukraine in the company of women in traditional dress. The crowd are watching a makeshift horse-drawn chariot race.

Kharkov tightly from west to north. Conditions inside the city are to be reconnoitred. Opportunities to seize the city by a coup are to be utilised.'

The northern role was assigned to the *Leibstandarte* and *Totenkopf*, with *Das Reich* attacking from the west and south. Resistance was light; Hausser felt sufficiently confident to take Kharkov by direct assault. On 11 March, one battalion from *Totenkopf* joined *Leibstandarte* and *Das Reich. SS-Brigadeführer* Fritz Witt of *Leibstandarte* put in a two-pronged assault with 3rd

Left: In June 1942 the *Leibstandarte* were withdrawn from the Eastern Front and sent west in anticipation of a possible Allied invasion. The photograph shows their barracks (complete with SS banner) during this period of refitting.

SS Battalion in the van, cutting the Kharkov–Byelgorod road. The *Leibstandarte* went in, together with the 22nd SS Panzer Grenadier Regiment. Late on the afternoon of 15 March, four days after 'Panzer' Meyer's battalion had gained the eastern edge of town amid bitter, house-to-house fighting, the last of the Soviet resistance crumbled. Kharkov once again belonged to the Third Reich. With his characteristic opportunism, Goebbels geared his Propaganda Ministry to declaim:

'In Poland and in France, in Greece and above all in the endless expanses of the east, the *Leibstandarte* has stood in battle, and the same men have committed themselves with arms for the National Socialist Greater Germany, who, even before 1933, strove in the black *Schutzstaffel* for the victory of the National Socialist movement.

'That their *Obergruppenführer*, their soldier of the First World War, the fighter of November 1923, the loyal companion of the Führer, the old SS leader and present general of the *Waffen-SS*, who exactly ten years ago set up the *Leibstandarte* and commanded it as a Regiment and now as a Division in the field, was today decorated with Oak Leaves with Swords, is their greatest joy and greatest pride.'

CALM PERIOD

After Kharkov, a period of relative calm ensued. It was then time to contemplate renewed offensive operations in the summer of 1943. The reconquest of Kharkov was rightly regarded as a considerable triumph, but the cost had been 11,000 dead for the SS Panzer Corps and 4500 for the *Leibstandarte*. The *Wehrmacht*, still under the shadow of defeat at Stalingrad, argued for a period of defensive warfare, with emphasis on lightning local attacks designed to wear down the Soviet army. But Hitler had been brooding long hours over his maps, extolling at his daily conferences the need for the grand flourish which once and for all would annihilate the enemy. If this were not done, the Führer declared, Soviet troops could well achieve a clear route to the Ukraine and thence to be able to sweep the Germans out of the Crimea.

There were other considerations beyond Europe. Defeat for Germany was looking probable, not least in the Navy (*Kriegsmarine*) where, in May alone, a total of 43 U-boats were lost against a monthly launching rate of 15. In North Africa, Field Marshal Erwin Rommel's Army Group Africa was facing a critical supply situation. Hitler, shuttling between his military compound *Wolfsschanze* (Wolf's Lair) in the gloomy Gorlitz forest, and the Berghof, his mountain retreat in southern Bavaria, searched for the source of the victory he so badly needed. As he pored over his maps, his attention fastened on a vast section of the Eastern Front fighting line. This was an area which extended north from Belgorod, lying north-west of Kharkov, to the distant area of Orel. In the centre was the Kursk salient, or bulge. Kursk itself was an industrial city with valuable coalmining, engineering and manufacturing centres.

KURSK

Intelligence sources had alerted Hitler to enormous offensive Soviet strength at this point, with a sterling input of field forces. In the words of von Manstein: 'The whole salient was just begging to be sliced off.' As the German planners saw it, there were two options. The first was a pre-emptive strike designed to hit the Soviets before they attacked. Alternatively, they could wait for them to move and launch a counterattack. The latter emerged as the most feasible. There would be a wait for the Soviet attack in the face of which ground would be given. The fallback would be to the River Dniepr, followed by a massive strike from around Kharkov, which would take the Soviet advance in its flank. Then would come cut-off and encirclement.

There was only one flaw. To Hitler, the merest hint of giving ground, even as the preface to a counterattack, was heresy. His refusal to have anything to do with such a proposal revealed the overall strategic

defects of this corporal–turned–supreme commander. While he possessed the scintillating talent for conceiving the grand flourish, there was also an inbuilt petulance of character, which expressed itself in fury at the mere suggestion that the detested Russian hordes be allowed any gains whatsoever at the expense of his forces.

This weakness was next compounded by doubt and dithering. Hitler confessed to Guderian: 'Whenever I think of this attack my stomach turns over.' Guderian was blunt: 'Leave it alone!' Finally, however, Hitler was not to be dissuaded, even when it was pointed out to him that, if there *were* an Allied landing in Europe and the Kursk campaign went ahead, there would be no available forces to fill the gap.

D-Day, first proposed for 1 May, was altered to a succession of other dates before being fixed irrevocably for 5 July 1942; it was codenamed Citadel (*Zitadelle*). By then, there was a fresh threat to Hitler. A high-level encrypted intelligence report, compiled by a group of senior *Wehrmacht* officers on 2 July, had reached Lieutenant General M. E. Katukov, the commander of 1st Tank Army. It contained nothing less than full details of the anticipated German attack, including its date. The Soviets were indebted to ULTRA, the intelligence source in Britain derived from the interception and decryption of German coded signal traffic. In addition, valuable material had reached a German emigré and anti-fascist named Rudolph Rössler, codenamed 'Lucy', who worked out of Lucerne and had contacts at the highest level within Stavka, the Soviet Supreme High Command. This advantage, as well as the delay in launching Citadel, enabled the Russians to set about constructing a deeply armed system of fortifications and minefields. Recruitment, too, was up; the strength of the Red Army was bolstered by the delivery of 6000 armoured fighting vehicles.

The weeks leading up to Citadel were significant for the *Leibstandarte*; Sepp Dietrich, his men learnt, would not himself be taking part in the Kursk offensive. On 4 June, he handed over command to *SS-Brigadeführer* Theodor Wisch, an SS high-flier still in his early thirties. From Berlin, Sepp Dietrich set about activating a new command, I SS Panzer Corps. Its creation had sprung from Himmler's desire to bolster his power and his influence by arguing for still further expansion of the *Waffen-SS*. The *Reichsführer-SS* insisted that new blood should be drawn from the *Hitler Jugend*; discussions were soon in progress between *Reichjugendführer* Artur Axmann and the SS leadership. It emerged that elements of the *Leibstandarte* and the SS Panzer Grenadier Division *Hitler Jugend* (later 12th SS Panzer Division *Hitler Jugend*) would constitute I SS Panzer Corps, with Hausser's corps being demoted to II SS Panzer Corps.

Below: German panzers during the Kharkov offensive in the spring of 1943. The success of Manstein's counterattack was a much-needed boost to German morale after the disaster of Stalingrad that winter.

The *Leibstandarte* would supply the officers and senior non-commissioned officers.

DIETRICH PROMOTED

As for Dietrich, an entirely new rank was created specifically for him. He became *SS-Obergruppenführer und Panzergeneral der Waffen-SS*. It was a promotion that came in the midst of a personal crisis. Dietrich – and he was not alone in this – was thinking the unthinkable: given the sheer numerical superiority in men and material possessed by the Soviets, he was edging towards the view that a decisive victory by Germany in the east was no longer possible. As he was not a man to muffle his opinions, Dietrich's reservations reached Himmler. Such was the extent of Dietrich's prestige, however, that the *Reichsführer-SS* felt he could only issue the following written rebuke: 'Whatever you

think about the war in the east, I know best ... We are sure the Russians can and will be defeated.'

As for Citadel, Hitler's plan was a classic pincer operation, moving from the north and south, both jaws heading to meet at a point east of Kursk. The thrust against the northern flank of the salient was to be carried out by General Walter Model's 9th Army – seven infantry and eight panzer and panzer grenadier divisions – while the southern flank belonged to General Hermann Hoth's 4th Panzer Army. As far as armament was concerned, the Germans threw in everything they had, greatly exceeding their resources at the start of the Russian campaign. The battle plan of Marshal Georgi Zhukov was sizing up to be an aggressive defence. This involved forcing his enemy to make the first move. When the Germans were worn down, counteroffensives would follow. No less than 40 per cent of the Red Army's entire infantry

Above: *SS-Standartenführer* **Fritz Witt (cigar in mouth) at Kharkov in March 1943. In recognition of his courage and conspicuous powers of leadership, Witt was later elevated to command the 12th SS *Hitler Jugend* Division.**

and armoured divisions was to implement the plan. An extra 50,000 men were kept in reserve. General Konstantin Rokossovsky's Central Front would defend Kursk's northern side, while the Voronezh Front of General Nikolai Vatutin would be responsible for the south.

As the date for Citadel grew ever closer, the Germans massed their forces: 50 divisions, a total of 900,000 men, with a further 20 divisions in reserve, plus 2700 tanks, including Tigers and Panthers. In its advance to the salient, the SS Panzer Corps, as part of 4th Panzer Army with a tank strength of 343, was to penetrate the first defensive belt via Beresov village

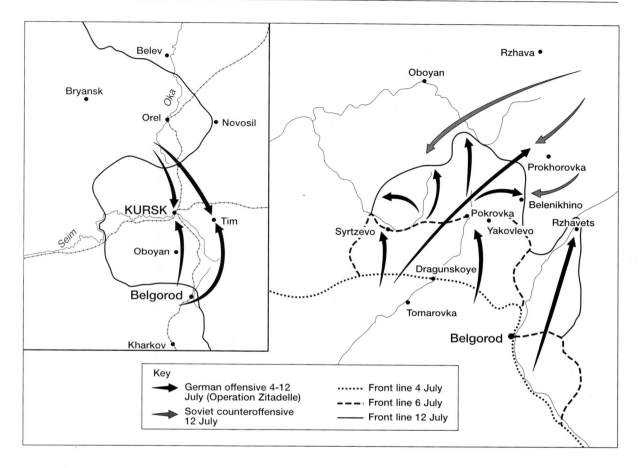

Key

→ German offensive 4-12 July (Operation Zitadelle)

⇒ Soviet counteroffensive 12 July

······· Front line 4 July

– – – Front line 6 July

——— Front line 12 July

and Sadeynoye. At Beresov, flame-throwing units were to head the panzer grenadiers, fighting their way in. Beyond lay the second belt between Lutchki and Jakovlevo. For the operation to the north-east, 167th Infantry Division, as part of SS Corps, had the task of guarding the left flank. The corps was a coiled spring.

WAITING TO BEGIN

One *Leibstandarte* man wrote: 'For reasons of security we have not been allowed to move about during the daytime and you can understand how hard this is, but now the waiting is over … It is cold black outside the Command bunker. Black clouds cover the sky and the rain is streaming down … The barrage has just begun. I can feel its force even down here deep in the earth.'

Above: Two maps, showing (left) the overall plan for Operation Citadel (*Zitadelle*), the attack on the Kursk salient, and (right) the southern prong of the attack, in which *Leibstandarte* took part.

During the Russian summer, dawn speedily sees off the night, so at 0330 hours on 5 July 1943, Operation Citadel began. It was destined to last for six hours. Another *Leibstandarte* man recorded in his journals: 'I saw our leading Tiger sections roar away and vanish almost completely in the peculiar silver/grey tall grass which is a feature of the area … Our mine lifting teams mark the position of Ivan's mines by lying down alongside them, thus using their bodies to mark a gap in the field. There are thousands of mines all over the area.'

The rapid advance of the *Leibstandarte* was exhilarating, with the first defensive positions falling easily and the tank squadrons encircling and wiping out the enemy. This did not last. All too soon there was the full force of the massed heavy artillery of the Russians and their tight network of exploding mines to be faced. The day belonged equally to tank men and foot soldiers. Of the former, *SS-Obersturmführer* Michael Wittmann, in the turret of his Tiger with its five-man crew, knocked out a clutch of T-34s with his platoon. An indication of the extent of the *Leibstandarte*'s collective adrenalin – to say nothing of its early arrogance – was afforded when Wisch made a sudden appearance near the Tigers and was greeted by one of his commanders with the words: 'Lunch in Kursk!' By the end of the day, Wittmann had claimed eight enemy tanks and seven anti-tank guns had been knocked out. It was not his only achievement.

Wittmann's Success

Barely an hour later, as his Tiger engaged anti-tank guns, Wittmann's crackling radio was telling him that the company's *Wendorff* platoon was in deep trouble. All at once, his Tigers were plunging through the nearby copse, only to come up against the rear of another Soviet anti-tank strongpoint. *Wendorff*'s plight was to be surrounded by a clutch of T-34s, which had put paid to one of the platoon's Tigers. Wittmann, spirits riding high, sped to the aid of *Wendorff*. Three T-34s were knocked out. The bag for the day was eight enemy tanks and seven anti-tank guns destroyed.

By no means all the SS men felt the same relish. *SS-Sturmann* Gunther Borchers of the *Leibstandarte* recorded in his diary: 'I am in a flame-throwing team, and we are to lead the Company attack. This is a real suicide mission. We have to get within 30 metres [90ft] of the Russians before we open fire. It's time to write out the last will and testament.'

The foot soldiers fought their way across the minefields and troughs to the first Soviet trench lines, where there were belts of trenches protected by barbed wire and minefields. There was hand-to-hand fighting with grenades, machine pistols, rifles, bayonets and occasionally trenching tools, employed to cleave the skulls of the enemy. As for the minefields, their density was such that a German corps could find itself lifting as many as 40,000 mines in a single day.

The second day of Citadel saw postponement of the *Leibstandarte* thrust until the afternoon because of bad weather. The dug-in tanks of the 1st Red Tank Army then came up against flame-throwers and constant counterattacks. The High Command War Diary of 6 July was scarcely cheerful; the element of surprise had not been achieved and there had been no decisive breakthrough. This meant that both flanks of the SS Corps were now open to Soviet counterblows. True, the War Diary was claiming, on 8 July, that 400 Russian tanks had been destroyed, but another entry revealed that the SS Corps had only 400 Panthers still operational out of the original 200. Many members of the tank crews, facing their first battle, fled their machines in terror to take refuge in the trenches from a fire which would barbecue them.

A fundamental fault lay in the panzer arm itself. The Tigers, despite their considerable power and 88mm (3.46in) guns, were lumbering leviathans with a cross-country speed of barely 19kmph (12mph) and an operation range of 96km (60 miles). The Ferdinands, heavy tank-destroyer Tigers with a vast thickness of armour, suffered from weak suspensions which frequently immobilised them, while the remote-control demolition Goliaths were not up to the job. It was the Soviet T-34, however, which had provided the Germans with their greatest shock. The German tank crews reported its agility in comparison with the Tiger and, along with other Soviet tanks, its speed in climbing slopes and swamps. A big advantage enjoyed by the Soviets was that the T-34 was in mass production; heavy losses were therefore of less consequence than they were to the Germans. This was to be particularly so during the battle of Kursk, where the High Command War Diary was to record the destruction of 663 Soviet tanks, a figure greater than the loss to the Germans. While Russian losses were replaceable, however, the losses of the Germans were irrevocable.

Above: A *Leibstandarte Sturmgeschutz* (assault gun) III or StuG III seen at Kharkov in the spring of 1943. The StuG III was used in both a support and an anti-tank role, the latter increasingly important as Soviet tank numbers grew.

Attack by *Leibstandarte* in a northeasterly direction along the Teterevino–Prokhorovka road, south-east of the River Psel, had been marked by some impressive achievements. *Obersturmführer* Rudolf von Ribbentrop, commander of No. 6 Company of lst SS Panzer Regiment and son of the German Foreign Minister, had faced 154 T-34s and a Soviet infantry battalion advancing between Prokorovka and Teterevino. The troop had lost three machines out of seven, with fighting taking place at less than 180m (200yds). It succeeded in clearing a path through the

Soviet area on the route to Oboyan, which lay some 60km (37 miles) from Kursk. But the capture of Prokhorovka, to the south-east of Kursk, proved an impossibility, both because of strong enemy resistance and the seas of mud created by the driving rain. Just to the south, the Soviet 5th Guards tank army mounted its furious assault. Hope centred on 3rd Panzer Corps of Army Detachment *Kempf*, which had a vital role in protecting Hausser's right flank; however, it failed to appear. On 10 July, the Soviet Voronezh Front, with a force of 10 corps, went over to the counteroffensive. On the plain to Kursk's southeast, two mighty tank armies deployed for what, up to that time, was the greatest tank battle in history.

Lieutenant General Pavel Rotmistrov, of the Soviet 5th Tank Army, clashed with the *Leibstandarte* at 0400

Above: *SS-Obersturmführer* **Michael Wittmann, foremost German tank commander of World War II, credited with 138 tank and assault gun and anti-tank kills on both fronts. He was killed near Caen on 8 August 1944.**

Left: Huddling in the holes they have dug to protect themselves against Soviet shelling, men of the *Leibstandarte* **wait for the order to attack again over ground that had been heavily fortified by the Red Army.**

hours two days later. A regiment of T-34s was annihilated. The main clash came just outside Prokhorovka, where Rotmistrov viewed the battlefield from a nearby hill. He later wrote: 'The tanks were moving across the steppe in small packs, under cover of patches of woodland and hedges. The bursts of gunfire merged into one continuous, mighty roar. The Soviet tanks thrust into the German advanced formations at full speed and penetrated the German tank screen. The T-34s were knocking out Tigers at extremely close range, since their powerful guns and massive armour no longer gave them an advantage in close combat ...

Left: The battle of Kursk was the largest armoured battle to date, with thousands of tanks and other vehicles committed to the fray. Although the *Waffen-SS* units made progress, their losses were heavy for the gains won.

Frequently when a tank was hit, its ammunition and fuel blew up, and torn-off turrets were flung through the air over dozens of yards … Soon the whole sky was shrouded by the thick smoke of the burning wrecks. On the black, scorched earth, the gutted tanks burnt like torches.'

Rotmistrov could have added that the tanks which thundered into the fray across the open steps were both Soviet and German, since each side charged at they knew not what, guns spitting furiously, even destroying their own side. Theorists of tank warfare said one of the prime tactical rules was that the panzers should exploit enemy weakness, not pitch tank against tank. The rule book was blown into oblivion.

Along with it went the concept of *Blitzkrieg* as a long, continuous sweep capable of bypassing even the strongest defences. *Blitzkrieg* was dead, along with Citadel itself. German losses were put at 70,000 killed or wounded, 3000 tanks, 1000 guns and much other war matériel. Soviet losses were not revealed. In Moscow, impatient queues formed for newspapers and the headlines were exultant. Among the most memorable was 'THE TIGERS ARE BURNING'.

After the war, Guderian reflected: 'The armoured formations, reformed and re-equipped with much effort, had lost heavily in both men and equipment, and would now be unemployable for a long time to come. It was problematical whether they could be rehabilitated in time to defend the Eastern Front; as for being able to use them in defence of the Western Front against the Allied landings that threatened the next spring, this was even more questionable. Needless to say, the Russians exploited their victory to the full.'

There were to be no more periods of quiet on the Eastern Front; now the enemy undisputably held the initiative. In the east, the Germans had ceased to be the hammer and had become the anvil.

CHAPTER SEVEN

CHERKASSY

After Kursk, the steamroller advance of the Soviets pushed 75,000 Germans into a pocket near Korsun and Cherkassy. The *Leibstandarte* were tasked with the role of relieving the besieged troops, pitting their limited resources against the ever-growing Soviet strength.

In the face of looming disaster which even Hitler at his most blinkered could not ignore, von Manstein and von Kluge were summoned to his headquarters in East Prussia to deliver a report on Operation Citadel (*Zitadelle*). Von Kluge was despondent: far from making a breakthrough, 9th Army had lost 20,000 men and was having to withdraw mobile troops to stem the advance of the Russians to Orel, which was threatening his rear. Von Manstein retained some optimism, believing that advances by 4th Army could still be made in the south. He argued that there was plenty of work still to be done, following attacks by the Russians against the Bryansk–Orel railway. It would take two divisions to stem the withdrawal. On 13 July 1943, Hitler was obliged to suspend Citadel.

The root cause for the halting of his incursion into the Kursk salient was the landing by the Allies of 160,000 men and 600 tanks in Sicily on 12 July 1943. Italian resistance in Italy was near collapse; Benito Mussolini had been overthrown and a new government was putting out feelers to the Allies about

Left: A *Schutzenpanzerwagen* (SdKfz 251/1) half-track armed with an MG34 machine gun in the snowy wastes of the Soviet Union. After defeat at Kursk, the remainder of the war would be one long German retreat in the east.

peace. Hitler therefore felt impelled to strengthen his grip on Italy. Troops were sent rushing up the Alpine passes. Hitler wanted the transfer of the *Leibstandarte* to Italy, as well as the entire I SS Panzer Corps.

OPPOSITION

To the commanders of Army Groups Centre and South, operating in the most vulnerable sectors of the Russian front, the prospect of losing any forces was anathema. Von Kluge, as Commander of Army Group Centre, was vociferous in his disapproval, as his exchanges with Hitler, which are on record, clearly demonstrate: 'What use can an elite SS Corps have sloping about the Italian lakes when there is serious work to be done here?' Hitler set out his reasons with uncharacteristic mildness: 'The point is, I can't just take units from anywhere. I have to take units that are politically reliable. It is a very difficult decision, but I have no choice. In Italy I can only accomplish something with elite formations that are politically close to fascism. If it weren't for that I could take a couple of army divisions. But as it is, I need a magnet to gather the people together. I must have units there which come under a political banner.' Further opposition came from Field Marshal Rommel, but even his prestige in the eyes of Hitler counted for nothing.

Left: Elements of the *Leibstandarte* trudge wearily past a row of burning houses in southern Russia during the general retreat after Kursk. From now on the war on the Eastern Front would be a series of rearguard actions.

In the event, a compromise was reached. Hitler consented to transfer solely the SS Panzer Group headquarters and the *Leibstandarte*, with the latter to leave the bulk of its armour behind. *Das Reich* was to remain with Army Group South. Snatched away from the Russian front, the *Leibstandarte* was to help stem the threat of a fall of the entire Italian peninsula. The 1st Company detrained at Jenbach, near Innsbruck, on 4 August 1943. Thence a fleet of vehicles took the men through the Brenner Pass, first to Bozen where, according to a postwar history of 1st Company, it received 'a triumphal reception' from the South Tyroleans. At Parma, 1st Company bivouacked, then embarked on training, guard and security duties. In the wake of the Italian's negotiated peace with the Allies, the tank barracks at Parma were occupied and the Italian soldiers disarmed. There followed a brief period of leisure in Trieste, where, according to one account, 'we used our free time to tour the city to take photographs and to get a haircut'.

GUARDING THE ALPS

Hitler's fear that the new government of Marshal Badoglio might seize the pass through the Alps accounted for elements of the *Leibstandarte* being placed at the Brenner Pass, while to the south, Dietrich's headquarters were sited at Merano in a defensive role.

These were not the *Leibstandarte*'s only duties in Italy. In the wake of Mussolini's fall, there occurred a diversion that was bizarre, even by the standards of Dietrich's ready-for-anything guard. Mussolini had been spirited out of Rome by order of the Badoglio government, moving from one prison to another. Despite the deteriorating situation on the Eastern Front, Hitler took time off to breathe life into his former ally, by now little more than a political corpse. He declared: 'I will never permit my friend Mussolini to be handed over to the Allies.'

Above: Mussolini during his rescue from Gran Sasso. He was flown to Germany in a Fieseler Storch, the tailplane of which is visible in the photograph. Elements of the Leibstandarte were involved in his rescue.

Thus, in a spectacular rescue bid codenamed Operation *Eiche* (Oak) carried out by No. 1 Company of the 1st Battalion of the 7th *Fallschirmjager* Regiment, the ex-Duce was snatched from the Campo Imperatore Hotel where he was being held. The hotel was atop the Gran Sasso d'Italia, the highest range in the Abruzzi Appennines and which could only be reached by funicular railway. Mussolini was delivered to Führer headquarters in Rastenburg, from there proceeding to the Lake Garda area to proclaim a short-lived Italian Socialist Republic. The charade also involved a company from a reconnaissance battalion and the flak battery from the *Leibstandarte*, who were given the task of defending Mussolini.

The *Leibstandarte*'s role did not end there. *SS-Brigadeführer* and *Generalmajor der Waffen-SS* Theodor Wisch, Dietrich's successor since the end of July as the *Leibstandarte* commander, received orders from Hitler to send an officer to escort Mussolini's wife Donna Rachele to Forli, south-east of Ravenna. This was a task undertaken by *Hauptsturmführer* Steinert, commander of the engineer battalion. From there, Donna Rachele went to Munich to be reunited with Mussolini and their children, before going on to Lake Garda. A further element of farce was added by the arrival in Lake Garda of Mussolini's mistress, Clara Petacci, who was installed in a villa nearby.

RECALLED TO THE EAST

On the Eastern Front, following the collapse of Citadel, the Russians pushed to the east bank of the

River Dniepr with four armies of the Second Ukranian Front, presenting a direct threat to the forces there. 1st SS Panzer Division *Leibstandarte SS Adolf Hitler,* now so designated, was recalled and 1st Company boarded trains for Ternopol and from there headed north in the direction of Kiev.

Army Group South had at its disposal 42 divisions, all badly below strength both in men and materials. Von Manstein, as Army Group South's commander, pleaded with Hitler to pull back forces forthwith to the Dniepr, shortening its front by a third. He argued that, with these savings, the Dniepr line, including approaches to the Crimea on the lower Dniepr, could be strengthened and held along a line which stretched from Zaporozhye to Melitopol, the so-called Wotan Line. Hitler was adamant that there must be no pullback and promised von Manstein four divisions from Army Group Centre; however, von Kluge could not spare them. The Russians pressed on swiftly towards Kharkov. The signs were that the city was holding out, but the presence there of XI Army Corps was a luxury von Manstein could not afford. On 22 August, he ordered the corps to pull out. The

following day, the city fell to the Red Army; the next threat was the Russian plan to take Kiev.

At this time came a fresh accusation of criminality against the *Leibstandarte.* Several mass graves in the area of Kharkov were discovered by the Russians. An investigation reported that: 'during the occupation of Kharkov and the Kharkov region, the German command and Gestapo agents savagely exterminated, by means of poisoning with carbon monoxide in *Dushagubbi* (murder vans), shooting and hanging, tens of thousands of Soviet citizens, including women, old men, children, wounded Red Army men under treatment in Kharkov hospitals, as well as arrested persons incarcerated in Gestapo prisons'.

Dietrich's men were among those accused and he himself was also singled out in a British Intelligence report as having probably fostered 'the worst type of Nazi thuggery' via the *Waffen-SS* and was dubbed 'an old SS beer-cellar gangster of Munich'. Even more grievous charges were levelled against Dietrich after the war regarding the Malmédy massacre, however, and his subsequent conviction by the Allied General Military Court meant that the Russians did not pursue the Kharkov allegations further.

On the Russian front, 4th Panzer Army, to whose XXXXVIII Corps the *Leibstandarte* was posted, was located in an arc south of Kiev, poised for a counter-attack against the southern wall of its salient. Before that, 4th Panzer Army was to strengthen the Army Group's northern wing. After closing the gap in the line, it would attack the flank of 38th Red Army, striking towards the agricultural region of Zhitomir, 130km (80 miles) west of Kiev. Then would come the annihilation of the Soviet bridgehead on the Dniepr's west bank.

The XXXVIII Corps attacked northwestwards and captured Zhitomir on 19 November, although this position was not able to be held for long in the face of Soviet pressure. In the short term, though, the

Left: Led by Joachim Peiper (centre), officers of the *Leibstandarte* lead some of their men on a march through an Italian town. The *Leibstandarte*'s stay in Italy was all too brief for the men; they were soon back in Russia.

objective of cutting the Soviet supply routes between Kiev and Zhitomir had been achieved.

BRUSILOV OFFENSIVE

The *Leibstandarte* concentrated next on the town of Brusilov where, although a strong Russian force was repelled by XXXXVIII Corps under General Hermann Balck, there was still formidable opposition from the Soviet's lst Guard Cavalry Corps and 5th and 8th Guards Armoured Corps. In the first tank offensive at this time, the *Leibstandarte*'s Michael Wittmann, dubbed the 'Panzer Killer', came into his own as indisputably one of the greatest of the German tank fighters, fulfilling everything expected of a *Leibstandarte* man. He destroyed six Russian tanks and five anti-tank guns before driving to the rear echelon to refuel and take on more ammunition. Another hero of the day was Reitlinger of the SS Self-Propelled Gun Battalion's No. 3 company who, while on reconnaissance, came face to face with 30 Soviet armoured vehicles. Attack was immediate: six of the tanks were destroyed and the rest driven off.

No quarter was given on either side in the tank war, as one SS Panzer Grenadier was to recall: 'Disengaging from the enemy ran fairly smoothly, but those Russian tanks which were fit for combat immediately pursued us ... Five T-34s with about 50 Russian infantrymen sitting on them came charging towards us. There was an exchange [of] fire ... The Russian tanks ... divided into two groups ... and then advanced on our column from the rear ... With that we were hopelessly surrounded. Some of our men surrendered at once and I saw [three senior sergeants] shoot themselves with their pistols ... I took cover in a potato field ... Night was falling. I heard the drunken hollering of the Russians and some pistol shots afterwards. I learned later that they were shooting my comrades in the back of the neck.'

Orders were given to the *Leibstandarte* for a two-pronged attack against the Brusilov concentration's western wall. At the same time, 1st Panzer Division had swept around the northern perimeter, attacking south with the objective of linking up with 9th Panzer Division. By 24 November, the encirclement was complete; the booty was 153 tanks, 70 pieces of artillery and 250 anti-tank guns destroyed. *SS-Obersturmbannführer* Jochen Peiper, commander of 1st SS Panzer Regiment, had gained the distinction of breaking through the Russian front and capturing the staff of four divisions.

But crippled by weak manpower, a bid by the corps to strike at the right flank of the Zhitomir–Radomyshl positions, which ran from the east to the southeast of Kiev, was a failure. The overall situation was not helped by a sudden rise in temperature at the end of November, during which roads were turned into quagmires.

SOVIET FORCES

The Soviets could command four Russian Armies, plus two independent corps mustered at the Kiev bridgehead with its depth of just under 80km (50 miles) and a width of nearly 190km (120 miles) – it was a front, moreover, that was pushing back the German forces. There was a drive by Wittmann's Tigers on the Teterev River at a point lying north of Radomyschl, where the Soviets were pushed back to the east bank. At the village of Golovin, Wittmann had the distinction of destroying his 60th tank, but overall progress was slow. Predictably, the weather proved fickle.

With the Germans facing blinding snowstorms and intense cold, Soviet forces marshalled for a renewed thrust in the direction of Zhitomir from the southwest. On the morning of 16 December, the *Leibstandarte*, controlling the armour of 1st Panzer Division, advanced eastwards, keeping to the line of the Irscha River with the ultimate aim – along with 7th Panzer Division – of surrounding the Soviets around Meleni. At first, surprise achieved a breakthrough of the Soviet defences but, in the face of the destruction of 46 tanks by the *Leibstandarte*, resistance strengthened. A fresh offensive by Army General Vatutin reached the Kiev–Zhitomir Road, a front of 29km (18 miles). Zhitomir was taken by the Soviets, along with the large supply dumps and foodstuff depots of 9th Panzer Army.

On 6 January 1944, Vatutin's columns struck southwards towards the Dniepr bend, virtually ignoring the severely weakened Panzer Corps, whose strength stood at fewer than 200 men per division. Within eight days, the *Leibstandarte* was battling fiercely around the areas of Zhitomir, Korosten and Berdichev. The division faced a mass of Soviet armour, dominated by T-34s and Klementi Voroshilovs (KVs), 16 of which fell to Wittmann in a single action, while Kling, commander of the Heavy Tank Company, put paid to 343 Soviet tanks, eight assault guns and 225 heavy anti-tank guns. The 1st Red Tank Army had breasted the Bug River, facing an attack from the SS in the Vinnitsa area which cost them several of their divisions and a toll of 7090 tanks and self-propelled guns, along with 8000 prisoners. At Berdichev, there was a link-up with 1st Panzer Division and the Red Army advance was stemmed.

Above: Back on the Eastern Front, men of the *Leibstandarte* pose for a propaganda photographer. In reality there was little time for rest as the Soviet forces pressed home their attacks on the German line.

RETREAT

Such achievements were, however, short-lived and have to be weighed alongside the overall advance of the Russians, who had pushed back German units by as much as 160km (100 miles). One of the most significant of the Soviet initiatives early in January 1944 was a bid to smash German forces around the town of Kirovograd, an objective which was achieved in the face of heavy German resistance. By the start of February, elements of 1st Panzer and 8th Armies, which included the SS *Wiking* Division and the Belgian SS-staffed *Sturmbrigade Wallonie*, amounting to 75,000 men and their equipment, were encircled in a

Right: Troops sort through debris on the streets of Zhitomir, a town briefly recaptured from the advancing Red Army. It was a temporary victory in the long retreat through the Ukraine in the winter of 1943–44.

salient around Korsun and Cherkassy, which lay to the north of Kirovograd. Von Manstein was determined to open the pocket, but once again he had to face Hitler's inflexibility and the Führer's insistence that contact must be established with the beleaguered forces. There must be no question of withdrawal or break-out. It was the same old mantra: the Dniepr line must be held, no matter the cost.

MANSTEIN'S RESOLVE

All von Manstein's instincts were for swift action. Still all too vivid were the memories of Stalingrad, that classic example of 'too little, too late' where meagre relief preparations and too few forces had spelt disaster. The mood of urgency proved infectious: plans were put in place for a breakthrough and ultimate defeat of the encircling Soviet divisions. The front would then be free for the advance on and recapture of Kiev. The XXXXVI and III Panzer Corps were assigned to the operation, the latter reinforced by the *Leibstandarte*, who were tasked with smashing into the enemy rear, followed by the attack of the two corps to trap the enemy.

The entrapped men within the pocket were bolstered by what seemed a confident undertaking that, at most, they would have to wait five days. What that undertaking did not take account of, however, was the result of the poor weather between the River Dniepr and the River Bug. Here, the thigh-deep mud of the Ukraine meant that everything was swallowed up in a sea of filth and the luckiest people involved were the Soviet peasants, who merely withdrew to their stoves. On arrival in the field, the main task fell on the forces of 1st Panzer and the *Leibstandarte*, whose orders were to beef up the attack and remain constantly mobile. Bridgeheads were established across the Gniloi Tickich River, west of Boyarka lying south-west of Kiev. Once again, Michael Wittmann emerged as

**Above: A hardy workhorse, the *Panzerkampfwagen* IV
(SdKfz 161) was armed with a 7.5cm (2.95in) gun. It was
to survive in service until the very end of hostilities. This
example served with the *Leibstandarte* in early 1944.**

the supreme tank destroyer. In two days of early
February, he put paid to 13 tanks and vehicles,
bringing his score at that point to 107 enemy
machines destroyed. In another triumph, Jochen
Peiper, struggling under the chronic shortage of
petrol, had to make do with a small group of tanks
which drove, unsupported, into enemy lines, to put
100 tanks and 75 anti-tank guns out of action. The

capture of a forward supply unit furnished several
thousands gallons of precious fuel.

The attack went in on 11 February 1944. The
Leibstandarte was grouped with 16th and 17th Panzer
Divisions, making up the northern flank, while 1st
Panzer Division formed the southern. The Soviet
High Command was briefly caught unprepared, but
recovery was quick and the Soviets put in V Guards
Army Corps to confront the panzers. This had the
effect of cutting off the German relief force, with
both sides having to deal with the appalling weather
and road conditions, and fog becoming an added
hazard. Men, guns and armoured infantry carriers

counterthrust cut off the German relief force. The pressure was kept up even as the appalling weather conditions were forcing more and more vehicles to drop out. The *Leibstandarte* was on the extended northern flank, grouped with 16th and 17th Panzer Divisions and was forced to give ground. The 17th Panzer Division came up in support, but that meant leaving 16th Panzer on its own to continue the assault, something which proved impossible, even though the trapped men in the pocket were just 13km (8 miles) away.

BREAK-OUT

Contact by either of the divisions was plainly out of the question and Hitler consented to a break-out on the evening of 6 February. The encircled forces began the retreat, a slow-moving procession of 35,000 survivors, inching their way towards III Panzer Corps, south-west of Dzhurzhentsy.

A Russian eyewitness described those German forces fleeing as 'black on the hillside, their ranks breaking and gathering, great explosions scattering them as our shells fell among them, but somehow banding themselves together again to press on down the hill as our tanks and the SS spat at each other across the refugees'.

At the fast-moving Gniloy Tikich River, the Soviet tanks moved in for the kill, crushing those who had not fallen to the guns. *Leibstandarte* provided what covering fire it could; when it was all over, it was estimated that 30,000 had escaped from the pocket. The *Leibstandarte* went on fighting doggedly. On Height 246.3, some 3km (2 miles) north-west of Tinowk, II Batallion of 2nd Panzer Grenadier Regiment faced fierce attack. In protecting the open right front of the battalion, most of 6th Company perished. James Weingartner, in *Hitler's Guard*, describes the sequel: 'Four survivors then stood against 60 Russian infantrymen supported by three T-34s and quickly lost two of their number. The remaining two men, an *SS-Rottenführer* and an *SS-Sturmmann* held their ground, ultimately reduced to the use of their service pistols, until a battalion counterattack drove off the attacking Russians.'

had to move through rivers of mud. Marching was next to impossible because the mud pulled the boots off the men's feet. The tanks' clogged tracks became as hard as concrete in the frozen mud and release was only possible with blow torches.

The *Leibstandarte* was able to drive 32km (20 miles) inside Soviet territory, but the bearing of the attack had been misdirected and there was a switch eastwards to reach the divisions which were encircled. This was a change of tack the Russians had not expected. There was no time, however, to exploit any momentary weakness. The Soviet V Guards Armoured Corps confronted the panzers and their

Severely mauled and soon to be reduced in strength to scarcely more than a *Kampfgruppe* (Battle Group), *Leibstandarte* pulled back into the line northeast of Uman, which lay to the west of Kirvograd. Within weeks, the combat strength was 41 officers and 1118 NCOs and men. Von Manstein wrote: 'Our forces had finally reached the point of exhaustion. The German divisions … were literally burnt out … The fighting had eaten away at the very core of the fighting units. How could we wage effective counter-attacks, for example, when an entire *Panzerkorps* had only 24 Panzers ready for battle?'

The sadly weakened state of the *Leibstandarte* was further revealed early in March when 1st Ukrainian Front, under the direction of Marshal Georgi Zhukov, Deputy Director of the Red Army, thrust into von Manstein's left wing. In the vast arena

between the Pripet and the Carpathians, Soviet 13th Army wreaked havoc upon the infantry forces of the Germans' XIII Corps, while to the south Zhukov launched four armies which succeeded in rippling open the entire German front. In happier times, the *Leibstandarte* would have provided invaluable offensive muscle, but by now it could do no more than be defensive. In the Uman area came the storming armies of the 2nd Ukrainian Front of Marshal Ivan Konev, cutting through to the Bug. By 26 March, Soviet advanced guards had crossed the Ukrainian frontier.

Below: Another example of a *Leibstandarte Sturmgeschutz* III in the cold of a Russian winter. In this photograph, taken during March 1944, it is participating in a counter-attack in the Vitebsk area, north-west of Smolensk.

Above: This SS journalist wears both the *Kriegsberichter* (War Reporter) and *Leibstandarte* cuff titles and monogrammed shoulder straps. Propaganda efforts were redoubled once the war began to turn against Germany.

In the circumstances, a period of rest and refitting was the only option for the *Leibstandarte* which, on 18 April, quit the Eastern Front, moving into the former billets of 12th SS Panzer Division *Hitler Jugend* at Tournhout, near Beverloo in Belgium.

Josef Goebbels, as ever a supreme opportunist when it came to prospects for propaganda coups, seized on the possibilities presented by the arrival of these members of the *Leibstandarte* in Antwerp. Here, troops from the division were paraded through the streets in immaculate order, and their progress was covered by radio, film and the press ('*Leibstandarte* returns triumphant').

Elsewhere, however, was the real world. Führer Order of 3 May called for the requisition of weapons for the *Leibstandarte*, but there were not enough of them. As for materiél, the vehicles coming direct from the factories proved of questionable value because of the severe shortage of fuel. *Hitler Jugend* Division was discovered to be overmanned and some 2000 young grenadiers – with an average of age of 18 and not even basic training, but willing to work hard for their SS runes – were eagerly absorbed into the *Leibstandarte*. The new blood, however, left out of the account the plight of its superiors; officers and NCOs were seriously thin on the ground. Those who were battle-hardened were enduring desperate weariness after close on five years service. Nevertheless, it was they who were to serve as the nucleus for a rebuilt *Leibstandarte* in preparation for the anticipated invasion of Europe by the Western Allies.

CHAPTER EIGHT

NORMANDY

Withdrawn from the carnage of the Eastern Front to rebuild, the *Liebstandarte* were on hand to counter the long-awaited Allied invasion in the summer of 1944. However, as in the Soviet Union, not even the cream of the *Waffen-SS* could stop the Allied advance.

When Sepp Dietrich visited his old division at the close of 1943, *Leibstandarte* was undergoing substantial refitting. Its members were in a state of sheer exhaustion, availing themselves of much-needed rest. At the beginning of 1944, Dietrich took up command of I SS Panzer Corps to prepare for the widely expected Allied invasion from across the English Channel. His orders were to be ready for either enemy air landings or an unexpected amphibious landing between Antwerp and Cherbourg. His headquarters in Brussels were moved to the Paris area.

The *Leibstandarte*, although in readiness near Bruges, was not immediately involved in the D-Day invasion of 6 June 1944. When the invasion took place, the division was suffering from consequences of the German Army High Command's indecision. Field Marshals Rommel and von Rundstedt had disagreed as to how the enemy should be countered. Rommel was in favour of meeting the enemy on the beach and driving it back, whereas von Rundstedt, as Commander in Chief West, believed the landings should be allowed to go ahead before moving in. Von

Left: Sepp Dietrich examines a map of Normandy with his staff while civilian refugees flee from the fighting in the background. Dietrich had been taken by surprise by the Allied landings, which were expected further east.

Rundstedt's argument was based on the uncertainty as to where the Allied strike would occur; either at Normandy, or from the Pas de Calais, which was the shortest route from the British mainland.

SURPRISE LANDINGS

The eventual choice of Normandy, where the Allied landings began, took everyone by surprise, not least Sepp Dietrich, then in Brussels on a visit to Theodore Wisch and the *Leibstandarte*. The invasion plan of Field Marshal Bernard Montgomery was to capture swiftly the medieval university town of Caen, some 16km (10 miles) inland from the Anglo-Canadian landing beaches. This would enable him to push south and east out of the beachhead. As well as taking the town, it was necessary for the Allies to secure its commanding heights in an area which consisted of small fields bounded by stout, hedge-topped banks, the *bocage*. There were also stone villages, studded woodlands, orchards and narrow, high-banked lanes which tended to favour the defenders. Progress could be achieved by forcing the River Odon and, by reaching the high ground lying to its south, dominating the roads. Von Rundstedt, like Montgomery, was a believer in speed: 'In view of the known ability of the enemy to bite fast (*festbeissen*), the important thing is to annihilate the enemy as quickly as possible.'

Right: With smiles on their faces, these men from Dietrich's I SS Panzer Corps seem confident in the face of the Allied invasion. However the Allies' superior logistics and air superiority would soon tell against them.

Dietrich's orders were to counterattack from Caen, which had become the pivot of the Allied line. Once such a remit would have quickened the pulse of every *Leibstandarte* man. It was true that, among veterans such as Michael Wittmann and 'Panzer' Meyer, the old arrogance and panache survived, but for the bulk of the elite formations these were vastly different days.

At first, there was encouraging progress. British 6th Airborne Division had suffered under panzer attack. British and Canadian infantry casualties had mounted through the treacherous network of the *bocage*, where they faced the full force of German tanks, machine guns and Nebelwerfer multi-barrelled mortars. Elsewhere, the situation was different. A few miles west of the River Orne, which flowed through Caen, US troops had pierced German defences through the Aure river valley, south of which British troops attempted to skirt Caen.

ATTACK ON VILLERS-BOCAGE

Dietrich's counterstroke began at 1000 hours on 8 June. The attack went ahead, but delays and shortage of fuel meant that only the battle group of Panzer *Lehr* was available. For 21st Panzer Division to enter the fray at this time was out of the question: it had been forced into a defensive role. *Hitler Jugend* stood alone, but could achieve little in the face of Allied artillery fire and air supremacy. There was no *Luftwaffe* to offer support and fuel was eaten up as vehicles coped with the network of narrow roads fractured by streams and hedgerows. The *Leibstandarte*, as we have seen, had been badly mauled and at this stage had virtually to be rebuilt from stratch.

Of particular concern to Dietrich, though, was to be a gap on the left front of Panzer *Lehr*, which the British were keen to turn. On the route south for

the Allied forces lay the village of Villers-Bocage, south of Bayeux, where their tanks stopped for the night. The quiet of early morning of 13 June was shattered by the clank and roar of five Pz Kw MK VI Tigers. A lone Tiger rolled out of woods north-east of the village on the road to Caen. The moment had come for the *Leibstandarte* veteran Michael Wittmann, who was now company commander of

the Heavy Panzer Battalion 501. Ahead of the four crewmen, on the road leading out of the village (rising to high ground marked Point 213 on Allied maps) stood a mass of British vehicles, including Sherman Firefly, Stuart and Cromwell tanks, Bren gun carriers and half-tracks. To Wittmann's astonishment, many of the British crews were standing around and brewing tea.

Wittmann peeled off in the direction of the village, swiftly setting ablaze the four Cromwells in the main street. An attack on the column near Point 213 on the Allied maps followed, with the Tigers firing their 88mm (3.46in) guns against the tanks and their machine guns against the infantry. In less than five minutes, a further 23 British tanks fell to the Germans, with the carrier and half-tracks engulfed

in flames. Around 100 men of the 4th County of London Yeomanry and the Rifle Brigade were killed and captured. For Wittmann, it meant promotion to *SS-Haupsturmführer* and the award of Swords to the Knight's Cross. His action had been the saviour of 1st SS Panzer Corps which was, in the words of Dietrich's biographer Charles Messenger, 'in danger of being peeled back like the lid of a sardine can'. As it was, the worrying gap on Panzer *Lehr*'s left front had been plugged. This development, although it obviously pleased Dietrich, was tempered by the death in action of another *Leibstandarte* hero, *SS-Brigadeführer und Generalmajor der Waffen-SS* Fritz Witt. Witt was holder of the German Cross in Gold, the Infantry Assault Badge and the Oak Leaves, and a man whose latter distinction had been to mould into a fighting unit the 'Crack Babies' of the 12th SS Division *Hitler Jugend*.

Above: Dietrich in Normandy with Rommel prior to the Allied invasion. Despite a mutual respect, Rommel doubted Dietrich's abilities as a strategist and Dietrich refused to be in awe of the legendary 'Desert Fox'.

Although a loyal Nazi from the very early days of the movement, Witt had been no mere *Parteisoldat*, but a soldier's soldier admired by *Waffen-SS* and *Wehrmacht* alike. Pressure had built up on 1st SS Panzer Corps in the sector of Tilly-sur-Seulles, south of Bayeux. Opposition came from fighter-bombers and the firepower of the 380mm and 406mm (15in and 16in) guns of HMS *Ramillies* and *Nelson*, which were lying in the Bay of the Seine. A bombardment from these ships killed Witt at his divisional headquarters south-west of Caen. Dietrich's reaction is worth recording, as it serves as a striking illustration of the *Leibstandarte* ethos:

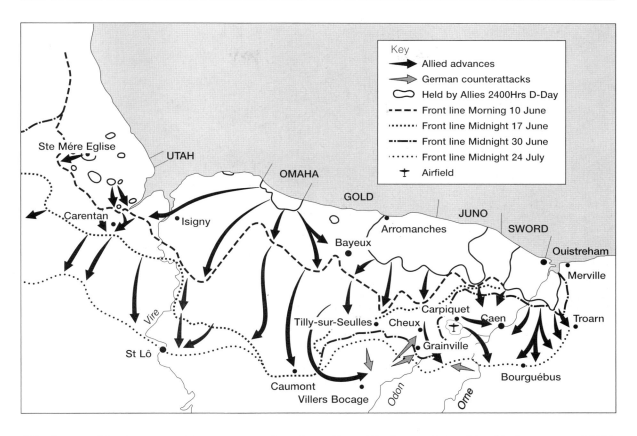

'That's one of the best gone. He was too good a soldier to stay alive for long.'

FIGHTING THE BRITISH

At the end of June, the *Leibstandarte* was back in action against the British advance into Caen and across the River Odon. Here it faced the 51st Highland Division, renowned for its tough professionalism, leading Sepp to comment: 'At last here's someone worth fighting.' However, German retaliation proved ineffective and it was not long before the British were pushing towards Falaise.

In the days following the D-Day landings, the Allies had maintained air superiority and the Germans had taken the brunt of it, their vehicles strung for many miles along the roads to Caen. On 4 July, the attacks on the division were stepped up, with the Canadians making a renewed bid to seize the Caen airfield at

Above: The Normandy beachhead in the summer of 1944. Although long-awaited, the location of the Allied landings caught most Germans by surprise, and the *Leibstandarte* had to move from their positions in the Pas de Calais.

Carpiquet. *Hitler Jugend* faced the might of the British 3rd and 59th Divisions. Held for 33 days by the SS, Caen was reduced on 7 July to little more than a heap of rubble, in one of the heaviest air attacks of the campaign. The attack, ordered by Montgomery, was intended as a prelude to his final effort to capture Caen in a front assault – Operation Charnwood, which was scheduled for the next day.

The original intention had been to take Caen on D-Day itself, but this was rendered impossible by the presence of a panzer division. Unless Caen was freed, men and supplies would not only be unable to move, but would also be sitting targets for air

attacks. This would entail the loss of infantry reserves, which the Allies could ill afford. Another consideration was that to the east of the beachhead lay the launching sites of Hitler's flying bombs, already attacking London. Destruction of these sites was considered a priority. Montgomery, spurred on by Churchill, who foresaw a haemorrhaging log jam at Caen, was keen to clear the town quickly. Operation Charnwood, the successor to an earlier initiative, Epsom, failed as a result of the Germans manning defensive positions within the ruins. Within 48 hours, it was called off.

GOODWOOD

The next initiative, Goodwood, was intended as a crack at the Germans with their substantial defences – four belts of natural and manmade obstacles and tanks held in reserve. *Wehrmacht* intelligence warnings, however, had already been issued. Dietrich later claimed that he learnt in advance about the attack simply by putting his ear to the ground, Indian-style, to detect the rumble of the oncoming British armour. The plan was for all four of the British and Canadian corps in Normandy to strike out for the Orne bridgehead to take the high ground of Bourguebus Ridge, overlooking the Caen–Falaise Road 6.5km (4 miles) to the south-west. Bourguebus village was held for a short time, but Dietrich's men recaptured it, while *Hitler Jugend* saw off the British armour, netting 400 tank casualties.

However, the manpower position remained dire. Since 6 June, lst SS Panzer Division had suffered 40 per cent casualties, while 12th SS Panzer Division *Hitler Jugend* losses stood at around 60 per cent. Dietrich, constantly nagging the SS Main Office, declared that such rates might have proved acceptable if there had been a likelihood of replacements. That was a prospect that grew increasingly unlikely, however, in the shadow of losses exceeding 100,000

Left: SS Panzer Grenadiers from the *Leibstandarte* are shown in this photograph watching anxiously as they take cover in a trench from an artillery barrage whilst in action in the Caen sector against the Canadians.

officers and men on the Western Front in the German armies generally.

On 20 July, *Leibstandarte* received devastating news unconnected to the fighting in Normandy and which reduced thoughts of battle to temporary insignificance. There had been an attempt on Hitler's life, subsequently revealed as unsuccessful, at the Führer's headquarters at Rastenburg in East Prussia. For a time, it looked as if the *Leibstandarte* might have been withdrawn and sent to Paris to deal with a faction of anti-Hitler conspirators there but in the event, the opposition in France came to nothing.

Five days later, at 0300 hours, 2nd Canadian Armoured Brigade in support of 3rd Canadian Infantry Division met with 1st SS Panzer Division at Tilly la Campagne. The Canadians had been thrusting towards Falaise, to the south-east of Caen, on the left-hand portion of the *Leibstandarte*'s sector, and had suffered considerable losses. At the same time, the Americans had launched their own break-out attempt with Operation Cobra in the Contentin peninsula. Largely because of bad weather and initially heavy casualties, Cobra started badly, but the Germans were soon at the receiving end of more than 5000 tonnes of high explosives and napalm. General Fritz Bayerlein commanding Panzer *Lehr* Division recorded that by noon, nothing but dust and smoke were visible and at least 70 per cent of his troops was 'dead, wounded, crazed or numbed …' The Allied 7th Corps attacked west of St Lô, the 8th between Périers and Lessay. Allied armour drove down the main road, carrying out vast encircling movements. Then, on 30 July, came a fresh disaster for the Germans with the fall of Avranches, west of the peninsula.

Hitler declared that the peninsula, along with Cherbourg to the extreme north, must be recaptured so as to split the US lst and 3rd Armies and annihilate them. On 2 August, the Führer ordered 'all available panzer units, regardless of their present commitment … to be taken from other parts of the Normandy front … and sent into a concerted attack'. He pinpointed the area of Mortain, east of Avranches. Von Kluge – now Commander in Chief West following the resignation of Von Rundstedt (whom Hitler had accused of

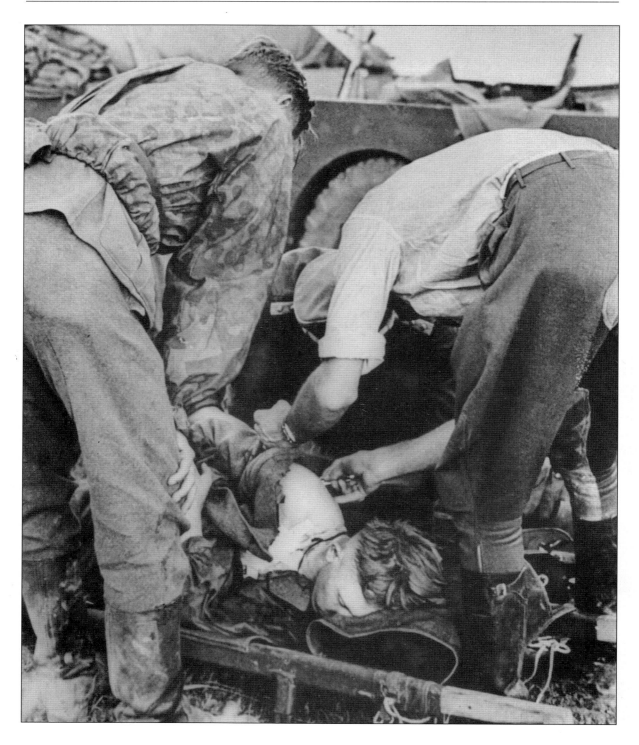

'defeatism') – reacted with a mixture of amazement and fury at the prospect of his panzers being diverted. This was nothing less than a threat to his entire front.

REACHING AVRANCHES

For Dietrich, in particular, Hitler's order came as a personal embarrassment. It coincided not just with his backdated promotion to *SS-Oberstgruppenführer*, but also the award of the Diamonds to his Iron Cross, to be bestowed personally by the Führer. Now was scarcely the time to raise the question of the state of the Normandy campaign. There was another factor. Dietrich was a realist: after the assassination attempt on Hitler, it was far too soon for him to be seen as in any way as lacking in loyalty. No individual opinion, still less criticism, could be voiced, lest it reach the ears of the SS and puppet elements of the *Wehrmacht*. If this was ignored, the perpetrator ran the risk of the notorious People's Court and the sentence of the garrot. Nevertheless, Dietrich did raise the issue, only to have it impatiently brushed aside during his interview with Hitler, which had lasted just two minutes.

The chance had been lost and the order stood: by 3 August, the *Leibstandarte* must withdraw from the British front and move south-east to the US sector. Von Kluge saw the attempt to reach Avranches as hopeless and was prepared to abandon it – a declaration which helped to put paid to a career already on the line. Hitler, possibly for the first time ever, levelled blame at the *Leibstandarte* for lack of commitment. There could, he made clear, be no question of abandoning the advance; indeed, the remnants of *Hitler Jugend*, south of Caen, were to be thrown into the fray. The new effort would be spearheaded by General Heinrich Eberbach's 5th Panzer Army (formerly Panzer Group West), now under Dietrich's temporary command.

All this, however, was to prove academic. Chester Wilmot, in *The Struggle for Europe*, wrote: 'In the

Left: A wounded Panzer Grenadier receives medical attention. A number of casualties to the *Leibstandarte* were caused by Allied shelling and air attack. Any obvious movement during the day would attract fighter-bombers.

remote fastness of his HQ in East Prussia, Hitler was living in a world of fantasy, sustained by optimism, ignorance and unrivalled capacity for self-delusion. He took no account of the exhaustion of his divisions, the parlous state of their equipment, the shortage of supplies or the impossibility of making large-scale movements by day. Even if none of these conditions had applied, his demands would have been difficult enough to implement in the face of the strength the Allies disposed, but Hitler did not understand that normal concepts of tactical time and space had been rendered invalid by Anglo–American air-power and mechanisation.'

The inexorable tide of events was tearing apart this cosy cocoon of delusion. In its continued attempt to reach Falaise, 1st Canadian Army struck again at an inevitably enfeebled 1st SS Panzer Corps. Morale and discipline cracked, as Kurt 'Panzer' Meyer recorded:

'Before me, making their way down the Caen–Falaise Road in a disorderly rabble, were the panic stricken troops of 89th Infantry Division. I realised that something had to be done to send these men back into the line and fight. I lit a cigar, stood in the middle of the road and in a loud voice asked them if they were going to leave me alone to cope with the enemy. Hearing a divisional commander address them in this way, they stopped, hesitated and then returned to their positions.'

The move, undertaken in foggy conditions, proved a gift to the Allied fighter-bombers who harassed the departing columns. Hitler's hope was that the thrust to Avranches could be undertaken both by the *Leibstandarte* and by *Hitler Jugend*, but 'Panzer' Meyer's division remained pinned down. Meyer had at his disposal just 500 men and a scratch assortment of tanks, which had been assembled on the Caen–Falaise road, running north to south. Meyer faced the Canadians who, fighting alongside Poles, reduced his manpower to a bare 500 men and 16 tanks. Nevertheless, in the short term, he had managed to stem the advance of the Canadians on the River Laison.

Dietrich was quick to contact von Kluge, who was told that, once the Canadians resumed the attack, Falaise could not be held for long. Paul Hausser, in

control of the 7th Army, joined with General Heinrich Eberbach in urging von Kluge to call off the attack. Von Kluge had received no instructions to do so, however, and was reluctant to commit such a flagrant act of disobedience. Eberbach, with 2nd and 116th Panzer Divisions and the *Leibstandarte*, had intended to strike in the fertile country region of Alençon, but he was too late and the town fell on 12 August. The advance was now on Argenten, which lay some 32km (20 miles) from the Canadians at Falaise.

Hitler was desperate for a counterstroke; to assist him in this manoeuvre, Eberbach received three more panzer divisions. However, the Canadians were also planning their drive there. Now under the command of *SS-Oberstgruppenführer* Fritz Kraemer, 1st SS Panzer Corps was chronically short of armour, which

Above: German materiel facing the advance of Allied forces in Normandy suffered a high rate of attrition. Here a German anti-tank gunner lies beside his weapon, with a knocked out Panther tank in the background.

rendered its infantry divisions totally impotent. Nevertheless, despite this, it did hold up escape by the enemy from the River Laison. Ultimately, however, it was useless; the Canadians made sure that there was no let-up, and succeeded in entering Falaise on the evening of 16 August. These were no longer the days when field marshals who were considered to have failed in their duty were told to take their batons into retirement. These men now faced the prospect of being deemed not merely incompetents, but also guilty of treachery.

In search of a scapegoat, Hitler fastened on von Kluge, who had been unwise enough to declare that Eberbach's counterstroke was impossible. During the Falaise debacle; von Kluge was caught in an Allied air attack and had taken refuge in a ditch, powerless to contact anyone. That he was out of contact, Hitler argued, pointed to him negotiating with the Allies. Hitler summoned Field Marshal Walther Model, who had gained prominence on the Eastern Front. As the replacement for von Kluge, Model was placed in command of the bed of nails that was the Supreme Command in the West. Von Kluge, ordered to report to Hitler and explain himself, took a cyanide pill on 19 August while flying between Paris and Metz.

Model's initial task was to gather what forces he could from Normandy and establish a new line west of the Seine. For Dietrich, his disillusion with the campaign in Normandy almost complete, his assignment from his new commander came as a bad joke: he was to be responsible for the new defence line from the Channel coast to the south of France. His immediate reaction was to ask with what was he excepted to accomplish this. The 7th Army – of which he was given command – with weak panzer grenadier units could barely summon 30 tanks in support.

PATTON UNSTOPPABLE

The Americans were by now seemingly unstoppable. At dawn on 20 August, Lieutenant General George S. Patton was announcing that he had crossed the Seine at Mantes-Gassicourt, less than 48km (30 miles) northwest of Paris. Attacks by the Germans within the new defence line were beaten back. Under continuous air and land attacks and faced with a lack of bridges and scant supply of ferries, setting up a front on the eastern bank of the Seine was plainly impossible. By the end of August, the British were in Amiens and, conceding that the war in Normandy was over, Hitler ordered Dietrich to report to him for a new assignment.

On 14 September, Dietrich learnt that he was to form the headquarters of 6th Panzer Army, consisting of I and II SS Panzer Corps, whose chiefs of staff were, respectively, *Generalleutnanten der Waffen-SS* Hermann Priess and Willi Bittrich. The *Leibstandarte* and *Hitler*

Above: Sepp Dietrich, 'Panzer' Meyer and other officers inspect new equipment which has been issued to the *Leibstandarte*. A wreath was added to the unit's insignia to mark Dietrich's award of the Knight's Cross with Oak Leaves.

Jugend were part of I SS Panzer Corps. Here, tried and trusted comrades were given appointments: Wilhelm Mohnke, a battle group commander in Normandy, was appointed *Leibstandarte* commander, with Fritz Kraemer heading *Hitler Jugend*.

The *Leibstandarte*, in common with the entire *Waffen-SS*, was a very different entity to that which had served Germany so well in previous years. Volunteers, however eager and dedicated, were not available in sufficient numbers. National Socialist ideology and strict entry standards, although still recognised, were an increasingly costly luxury in this war of survival.

The propaganda offensive was stepped up. A *Leibstandarte* leaflet proclaimed: 'The *Leibstandarte* has, in over five years of war, pinned success on its banners. And it has, along with these often decisive victories on all the battlefields of Europe, brought the greatest sacrifices in blood and life, and always stands, by the will of the Führer, where things are going hardest. We want to be the best … because one expects this performance from us and must expect it.'

Ethnic Germans were conscripted in ever greater numbers; Dietrich was expected to wield this untrained raw material into an effective panzer army. It was with this, and a chronic shortage of tanks and fuel, that Hitler prepared for a monumental gamble.

CHAPTER NINE

ARDENNES

The Allies stood poised to invade the German homeland. Hitler concentrated his entire reserves for a desperate gamble, a re-run of the 1940 attack through the Ardennes. The *Leibstandarte* was called on once more to perform a key role in the offensive.

Even with his physical and mental powers in irreversible decline, Adolf Hitler still possessed the one attribute that marked the habitual risk-taker – the ability to gauge a serious weakness in an opponent. As Supreme Allied Commander, General Eisenhower had found the going tough on the approaches to the German frontier lying west of the Rhine. In October 1944, the old imperial capital of Aachen had been secured by US 1st Army, the first German city to fall into Allied hands, but the Rhine had not been reached. Success for Germany, Hitler declared, must be achieved by a spectacular gesture.

Hitler had been nurturing a dream even as the German armies in late summer had been streaming home in defeat. Essentially, it amounted to a replay of 1940: once again, German armies would drive through the forests of the Ardennes to the Meuse, then sweep north for the seizure of Antwerp, which would deprive Eisenhower of his main port of supply. The operation was codenamed *Wacht am Rhein* but history has dubbed it, more prosaically, the Battle of the Bulge.

Left: Soldiers from the 6th SS Panzer Army pose for a propaganda film whilst smoking captured American cigarettes. Two Panzer Armies had assembled for the attack on an 80-mile (130km) front against only six American divisions.

In essence, Hitler proposed there should be an hour-long bombardment of the Ardennes section of Eisenhower's 1600km (1000-mile) front line – 'an earth shaking inferno'. That would be followed by an advance of infantry along a 96km (60-mile) front between Monschau, 40km (25 miles) south-east of Aachen, and Echternach in Luxembourg. A two-wave tank assault would be implemented through the woods and hills of the Ardennes to seize bridges across the River Meuse between Liege and Namur. The second wave would pass through to seize Antwerp. The Anglo-Canadian 21st Army Group and the left wing of the US 12th Army Group would be severed. There was no stopping Hitler's orgy of wishful thinking. It was likely, he argued, that the English and the Canadians would evacuate the southern Netherlands in a 'new Dunkirk'. The Americans would then abandon Europe and focus all their forces on Japan. The full strength of Germany could then return to engage the Red Army.

ARDENNES DISCOUNTED

Eisenhower had reasoned that the Ardennes, with its profusion of forests and deeply incised streams, was unfriendly to the thrust of mechanised armour, particularly with the depleted number of tanks it was assumed Hitler possessed at this stage of the war. The area of hilly forests was held on a 128km (80-mile) front by only six American divisions and officially designated a 'quiet sector'. Troops had thus been positioned for offensives over less forbidding terrain.

For the Germans, the drawback was a lack of personnel and armour. Hitler's vision impressed neither von Rundstedt, who by now had been reinstated as Commander in Chief in the West, or Model, as commander of Army Group B. Both argued that the entire operation was fatally impractical and the fond hope of returning to a full-scale foray in the east plain lunacy. Von Rundstedt later declared: 'When I received this plan early in November … It was obvious to me that the available forces were far too small for such an extremely ambitious plan.'

PREPOSTEROUS IDEA

After the war, von Rundstedt told the historian Basil Liddell Hart that he knew the scheme was so preposterous that he refused to attend a military conference to discuss the issue. He sent his Chief of Staff, General Gunther Blumentritt. At the conference, which Sepp Dietrich attended, it was argued that Antwerp was an especially dangerous choice; inevitably, the British and the Americans would mount counterstrikes against long, exposed flanks. An alternative was proposed to Hitler: an offensive would be limited to pinching off the American salient around Aachen. Predictably, opposition proved fruitless and Hitler's vision was adopted. His sole concession was to postpone the start date from 15 December to the 16th.

To Dietrich's 6th Panzer Army (later 6th SS Panzer Army) fell the major role as by far the strongest army in the Ardennes. It could command a mobile striking force of I SS Panzer Corps (comprising 1st SS Panzer Division *Adolf Hitler* and 12th SS Panzer Division *Hitler Jugend*) and II SS Panzer Corps (consisting of SS Divisions *Das Reich* and *Hohenstaufen*). Its task was both formidable and daunting: to break through the Monschau –Krewinkel sector, near the border between Germany and Belgium, then send its armoured spearheads across the Meuse south of Leige. After

screening its right flank on the Albert Canal, the drive would be on to Antwerp.

An avalanche of orders from the Führer emerged, minutely detailing everything from the initial artillery bombardment to methods of adapting tanks to spread grit on icy roads and the number of vehicles and horses needed for individual divisions. When von Rundstedt received the final orders, the words 'Not to be altered' were scrawled across them in the familiar spidery handwriting. As far as his temperament allowed, Dietrich kept his views on the assignment under wraps. Only after the war's end, while being interrogated by the Canadian Milton Shulman, did he give vent to long pent-up frustration:

'All Hitler wants me to do is to cross a river, capture Brussels, and then go on and take Antwerp! And all this in the worst time of the year through the Ardennes where the snow is waist deep and there isn't room to deploy four tanks abreast let alone armoured divisions! Where it doesn't get light until eight and it's dark again at four and with re-formed divisions made up chiefly of kids and sick old men – and at Christmas!'

But to Dietrich, a Führer order was precisely that. He marked the opening of the offensive with the declaration: 'Soldiers of the 6th Panzer Army! The great moment of decision is upon us. The Führer has placed us at the vital point. It is for us to breach the enemy front and push beyond the Meuse. Surprise is half the battle. In spite of the terror bombings, the Home Front has provided us with tanks, ammunition and weapons. They are watching us. We will not let them down.'

As it turned out, the early phase of the attack, through deep snow before dawn on 16 December, achieved short-lived advantage for 6th Panzer Army when some 83,000 Americans found themselves up against 200,000 German troops. An aid to the army's advance was Operation *Greif*, code name of a special brigade under *Standartenführer* Otto Skorzeny, which recruited German soldiers who spoke English with an American idiom and spread confusion and false intelligence amid the American rear positions. The scheme achieved a measure of success, before the

Above: These German supply vehicles ready for the offensive – which were increasingly few in number and bereft of sufficient fuel – additionally had to cope with the bleak winter conditions of the Ardennes in 1944.

availability of suitable Germans ran out, along with captured uniforms, converted equipment and vehicles. The fate of these ersatz Americans on capture was swift. They faced US firing squads.

Indisputably, the most formidable German force in the Ardennes was *Kampfgruppe Peiper* (Combat Group *Peiper*), under the command of 29-year-old *Obersturmbannführer* Jochen Peiper, former adjutant to Himmler, with his long record of combat experience and whose panzer grenadiers were designated the 'Blowtorch Battalion'. Its task now was to seize the Meuse crossings at Huy, which lay between Liege to the east and Namur to the west, with maximum speed.

The panzer group comprised 1st Panzer Battalion of 2nd Panzer Grenadier Regiment, SS Reconnaissance Battalion, artillery, anti-aircraft guns, Pioneers,

Left: A sorely-needed stroke of luck in the last months of the war. This Nazi film shows Germans during the counter-offensive in Belgium taking equipment across an engineer-built bridge captured from the Americans.

Engineers and Services, and some of Skorzeny's 'Americans'. Twelve panzers were disguised to look like American Shermans. The column, about 24km (15 miles) long, would move from east to west. On the direction itinerary mapped out personally by Hitler, movement was to be a constant flow, regardless of activity on the flanks. From Losheim, the route would lead west to Honsfeld and via Schoppen to a road junction at Baugnez. There would then be a southern turn to the south to Ligneuville, followed by a westward strike to Stavelot on the Amblève River, arriving at the village of Trois Ponts. A breather was permitted at Werbemont, followed by the dash for Huy, where the bridges were to be seized.

SPEED VITAL

The crucial requirement was speed: the river bridges had to be reached and crossed before being destroyed by the Allies. A good many of the roads were totally unsuitable for armour, an inconvenient truth to which Hitler gave no regard. Movement was not made easier by a succession of wooded ridges and deep river valleys. On the other hand, Antwerp could be reached by a road considered suitable for armour. Success depended on whether a break-out of the Ambleve river valley was possible on the few bridges sturdy enough for the heavy tanks. No consideration had been given by Hitler, who had traced out the route minutely, to the inescapable fact that this was totally unsuitable terrain for armoured vehicles: 'fit for bicycles', was Peiper's reported comment. Neither was the chronic shortage of fuel taken into account: commanders were expected to capture the supplies they needed from American dumps. To make matters even more difficult for Peiper, because of the deep secrecy surrounding his operation, any form of reconnaissance of the route was out of the question.

Above: Troops from Dietrich's 6th SS Panzer Army, shown interrogating the American prisoners they have captured. The SS soldier in the centre carries a *Panzerfaust* anti-tank rocket over his shoulder.

The troops received by 6th Panzer were initially organised into I and II SS Panzer Corps, under the commands, respectively, of the *Waffen-SS* generals Hermann Priess and Willi Bittrich. The 1st SS Panzer Division *Leibstandarte* was commanded by Wilhelm Mohnke, while Fritz Kraemer, Sepp's former chief of staff, received the *Hitler Jugend*. Priess was to make a breakthrough in the 11km (7-mile) wide rolling countryside of Losheim Gap, at the start of the route assigned to Peiper. Aided by a Parachute and *Volksgrenadier* ('People's Grenadier') Division, Priess would tear open the gap through which would pour Peiper's men, spearheading the advance. It was Priess who passed via Peiper to senior commanders the exhortation from Hitler; the offensive represented 'the decisive hour of the German people'. Accepted rules of war conduct were inapplicable and progress

was fuelled by revenge for 'the innumerable German victims of the bombing terror'.

The logistics involved in the movement of men and matériel to the front were formidable: 200 trains were required for the *Leibstandarte* division alone. By 12 December, all frontline positions had been taken up. The next day artillery arrived on muffled wheels. Icy, gale-force winds turned out to be a blessing, as the cold reduced activity on the American side and the wind drowned the clatter of the tank columns.

On Saturday, 16 December 1944, the day designated 'Autumn Fog', Peiper's group rolled: a total of 22

German divisions were facing four and a half US divisions. It soon became clear that adherence to an inflexible timetable, let alone a prescribed route, was impossible. A confused jam of army vehicles built up in the mud and snow on the approach to the Losheim Gap, situated just inside Germany and through which it was necessary to traverse a thick belt of woodland before open country a few miles deeper into Belgium could be crossed.

Peiper's column was halted abruptly. He was confronted by a tank minus its right track, which had slewed across the road. There were other tanks in the same plight: a smoking black hole indicated the presence of mines. There was no time to alert combat engineers to bring their detectors to the front of the column. Peiper, in a move which it was later revealed cost him six tanks and half-tracks, took the decision to clear the way by the simple expedient of rolling over the mined areas.

It was the same story when Peiper received orders to turn west and move through the village of Lanzerath, near the northern extremity of the Losheim Gap. Here, many US soldiers were lodging with local families and digging emplacement machine guns in the gardens. There were also, as Peiper discovered, anti-tank mines placed on the road leading to the village. The column was ordered to advance notwithstanding, which led to the loss of a further five vehicles. A switch was made to the primitive paths of the surrounding pine forests, so as to avoid the heavy artillery fire of the Americans on the road to the town of Stavelot. Next, after a fierce exchange with the commander as to the future role of the paratroopers in 9th Parachute Regiment, Peiper commandeered a whole battalion, mounting them on the tanks of his waiting column.

PEIPER'S PANACHE

It was a vintage example of the SS man's panache and it was by no means the last. On the approach to the small town of Honsfeld on the Buchholz–Honsfeld

Below: The pace of the German offensive in the Ardennes is clearly demonstrated in this propaganda photograph, with men of 6th SS Panzer Army crossing a road blocked by wrecked US equipment.

road, Peiper again found his progress hindered by a host of US vehicles and men retreating westwards. He waited until he saw a break in the columns and then coolly inserted the *Kampfgruppe* (combat group). The presence of two captured Shermans afforded concealment when he entered and captured the small town of Honsfeld. By this action, Peiper had thus managed to clear the route for the following *Leibstandarte*.

Below: More shots from a propaganda film showing members of 6th SS Panzer Army posing by burning American equipment. Unfortunately for the German propagandists, this particular film was itself captured by the Allies.

It was at this point that deteriorating weather and rapidly declining fuel supplies became chronic. If Peiper was to obey his Führer's orders to the letter, his advance would proceed via Schoppen, directly on the mandatory route. Road conditions, however, made progress for the tanks impossible – within the timetable, at any rate. To the north lay not only a road with a more satisfactory surface, but also, Peiper learnt, an American petrol dump at Bullingen which was within reasonable distance.

FORBIDDEN TERRITORY

Both the diversionary road and Bullingen were territory which Peiper had been specifically ordered to

Right: *Gefreiter* **Wilhelm Schmidt, a member of Otto Skorzeny's Operation *Grief* who posed as an American in order to spread confusion and false intelligence during the Ardennes offensive, faces a US execution squad.**

avoid. Nevertheless, he did not hesitate and 10th Company was detailed to reconnoitre. The petrol dump was captured, along with some sullen American prisoners who were mustered to fill the vehicles of the combat group. As an aside, at least one subsequent account of the seizure of the petrol supplies stated that a number of prisoners were shot once their task was finished. By midday, the column had returned to the official route, under fire from US artillery and enemy tanks which destroyed two Mark IV vehicles. Intent on carrying out a pincer attack upon the small town of Ligneuville, Peiper divided his column; a second detachment of tanks and grenadiers advanced on his right flank. At around 1300 hours, near the Engelsdorf Road inter-section, several miles south-east of the hamlets of Malmédy and Baugnez, Battery B of the US 285th Artillery Observation Battalion, 140-strong, ran directly into the point of Peiper's force which was moving west to Stavelot.

Accounts of subsequent events on 17 December – like the testimonies of survivors of the massacre of at least 86 American prisoners – are conflicting and con-fusing. What is indisputable is that machine guns from Peiper's half-tracks raked the trucks from which the American troops, many devoid of combat experi-ence, leapt so that they could take refuge in nearby ditches. They were quickly rounded up by panzer grenadiers riding on the tanks, disarmed and ordered to wait in a field by a roadside café until German troops, who were following, could take charge of them.

SLAUGHTER

Peiper's spearhead then moved in the direction of Ligneuville, on the road to Stavelot. At some point during this movement of half-tracks, motor cycles, tanks and self-propelled guns, fierce pistol and auto-matic fire from two Mark IVs poured into the defence-

less prisoners, along with the cry of 'Kill them all!' It was later alleged that one man responsible for the very early shots was an assistant gunner, *SS-Rottenführer* George Fleps, 21, a volunteer from Romania.

Second Lieutenant Virgil T. Lary of the US Army, together with his colleague Ken Aherns, who had been wounded twice in the back, later recalled that the cessation of machine-gun fire was followed by pis-tol shots, as the *coup de grâce* was administered. The SS men walked among the bodies to detect any sign of life, kicking them in the face and kidneys. On the nearby road, tanks ran over the bodies of those who had managed to escape from the meadow. During the afternoon, Colonel David E. Pergrin, whose US 291st Combat Engineer Battalion was defending Malmédy, heard machine-gun fire and shouting, before encountering four men stumbling out of the woods,

Right: Three men from Joachim Peiper's *Kampfgruppe* (combat group) peer at a road sign to check their progress towards their target on the Malmédy road. This photograph was taken during the Ardennes offensive.

who blurted out the first details of the massacre to reach the Americans. The next day, 1st US Army flashed the news to SHAEF (Supreme Headquarters Allied Expeditionary Force) and 12th Army Group. The order was given that the Malmédy massacre should be given the widest publicity.

At the same time as the snow was forming on the crossroads, shrouding the bodies, the survivors of Malmédy were being interviewed by two journalists, Hal Boyle and Jack Belden of the magazine *Time*. Before long, 328th US Infantry Regiment was issuing an order that no SS troops or paratroopers would be taken prisoner, but would be shot on sight. As for Dietrich, he claimed that poor communications left him in ignorance of the massacre until 21 December, when he was handed a transcript of a report from a radio broadcast from Soldatensender Calais, a British propaganda station run by the journalist Sefton Delmer. When questioned after the war, Dietrich denied receiving the transcript, conceding only that he had heard about 'some form of atrocity' around that time. Nevertheless, he had ordered an immediate investigation and, predictably, came up against a solid wall of denial.

BREAK FOR LUNCH

Both columns made it to Ligneuville and took time off to eat the lunch that had been prepared for the Americans, before pressing on to Stavelot where the bridge would prove a valuable prize as it could bear the weight of the Tigers. With just 60 grenadiers, Peiper, taking account of the fading light, pressed on with the assault, but there was a sharp riposte of rifle, machine-gun, artillery and anti-tank fire. Only 68km (42 miles) from the Meuse and overcome with exhaustion, the strung-out columns bedded down for the night. At first light on 18 December, the area of Recht was seized by grenadiers, but the mass of the

Leibstandarte Division was hopelessly strung out and clogging the rear areas.

Reinforcement was out of the question; Peiper took the decision to press on alone and there was a short, sharp barrage which enabled infantry and tanks to storm the Stavelot bridge and secure the southern half of the town after the stone bridge had been crossed. A plan to peel off a tank squadron to capture the vital river crossing of the Amblève valley at Trois Ponts came to nought when two of the bridges were blown up in the face of the panzers. However, at Cheneux, lying to the north-west of Trois Ponts, Peiper succeeded in taking a bridge intact. It was so placed that, if he were successful, there was still a chance of breaking out of the Amblève valley and reaching the Meuse. The skies and fog cleared, however, and there was the opportunity for attack from the air. Fighter-bombers of 365th and 368th fighter groups attacked. Although casualties were low, the resulting debris blocked the roads, and this caused further delay.

Once more there loomed the spectre of petrol famine; no fresh supplies had been obtained and those that were available were either unable to get through due to the air attacks, or were in insufficient quantity. A remote chance of breaking out of the Amblève valley was presented at Stoumont, a territory of open country and level, cultivated fields which lay to the north of Cheneux and which could be more accommodating to tanks. Peiper's resources included the King Tiger Battalion, which had joined him at Stavelot, a battery of 105mm (4.13in) self-propelled guns and a parachute company. With these resources, the battle began on 19 December.

At 0700 hours, the area was darkened by dense fog, a drawback which by no means prevented Peiper from pushing his panzers forwards in the face of what turned out to be a weak defence. By midday, Stoumont became a fleeting prize for the Germans. The station was not secured, however, a necessary achievement before it would be possible to push onto a bridge across the Amblève. Ten Mark IVs, which arrived in Stavelot along the road from Trois Ponts, hastened under cover from air attack. A Tiger from

501st Heavy Panzer Battalion was knocked out by a bazooka fired at close range.

LACK OF FUEL

By grim irony, Peiper had secured a bridge over the River Amblève. But it was an empty triumph: he had no fuel to cross it. Without help he was powerless to move. Then came the counter-attack at Stavelot, which the Americans took. Peiper sought permission to turn around and fight his way back to the rest of 1st SS Panzer Division. He was refused and ordered to stay where he was until the rest of the division were able to reach him and the drive to the Meuse resumed. Such reserve back-up, he was told, was unlikely to be available for at least three days. However, a battalion of 2nd SS Panzer Grenadier Regiment of 1st SS Panzer Division, moving for the most part on foot by way of a wooden span over the Amblève upstream from Trois Ponts and through railway underpasses, managed to reach Peiper. Furthermore, the battalion had been able to bring a small supply of petrol.

Scratch battle groups were formed as relieving columns, but penetration was limited to Wanne, south-east of Trois Ponts. By midnight, after a winter afternoon and evening of fighting, the *Leibstandarte* had reached the extent of its advance and was forced back and put in the line at St Vith, a vital road centre for supplies and reinforcements. The pattern from then on was one of withdrawal to the streets of the tiny hamlet of La Gleize, lying to the north-east of Stoumont.

The American seizure of Stavelot revealed that there had been an orgy of atrocities both in Stavelot itself and at Trois Ponts and the nearby hamlets of Parfondruy, Ster and Renardmont. At Stavelot, the slaughter of civilians, in revenge for harbouring US troops, could be laid at the door of *Kampfgruppe Peiper*, since its men were the first to pass through. Numbers given for those executed vary, according to which areas are cited for figures, but it is widely agreed that between 130 and 140 civilians had been killed in and around Stavelot alone in a single day. After the war, for these crimes and others, Sepp

Dietrich and Jochen Peiper, along with 70 men of his December 1944 *Kampfgruppe,* were consequently brought to trial (see the chapter on key figures of the *Leibstandarte*).

DESPERATE PLIGHT

An indication of the desperate plight which faced the panzer grenadiers was indicated by the decision to abandon armoured assault at Stavelot and, during the early morning of 20 December, send the panzer grenadiers wading through the icy waters of the Ambleve. According to the American Charles McDonald, who commanded an infantry company

Below: An empty fuel dump which once belonged to the American forces in the forest of the Ardennes. For the Germans, desperately short of fuel, the sight of these containers would have been a grim irony.

during the Ardennes offensive and subsequently wrote an exhaustive account of it:

'By the light of flares, American soldiers in the building facing the river had little difficulty picking off the men struggling through the water. Some concentrated their fire on those carrying makeshift ladders and on anybody who looked to be an officer, while supporting tanks fired white phosphorus shells in an attempt to light the scene by setting fire to houses on the other bank. When that failed, Sergeant William Pierce swam the river with a can of gasoline, emptied it against the side of a house, and set it afire.'

Those who did reach the opposite shore were given no quarter and shot down mercilessly. Such a measure by the Americans should perhaps be judged in the context of their fury at the atrocities committed against their fellow troops at Malmédy and the murder of civilians.

Left: Tagged for purposes of identification later on in the war, the American victims of the Malmédy atrocity lie in the snow exactly where they fell to the bullets of a contingent of the *Leibstandarte*.

Meanwhile, Cheneux, on the southern sector of the German salient, together with a nearby bridge, remained in German hands. The Americans faced the bulk of Peiper's light flak battalion, strengthened by 2nd Panzer Grenadier Regiment. In the ensuing action, 1st Battalion of 82nd Airborne Division's 504th Regiment sustained heavy losses from light flak fire. Many US troops fell victim to grenades and knife attack, which was repaid with interest and ultimate success, thus reducing the size of the bridgehead.

The Amblève river valley remained uncleared. For the Germans, the crossing of the Meuse was no longer on the agenda, any more than was holding Stoumont.

The prime concern was to extricate the existing forces of the *Kampfgruppe* from inevitable disaster; there would be a pullback to La Gleize, retaining what was left of the Cheneux bridgehead. The *Kampfgruppe* headquarters withdrew to streets and houses within La Gleize, where American prisoners and German walking wounded were mustered to cellars and put in the charge of a German medical sergeant and two American first-aid men. Peiper briefed his officers that the bulk of the *Leibstandarte* had been given the task of providing his men with an escape route involving an assault from the south on Malmédy, thus opening the road forwards to Antwerp.

Below: The progress of the German attack through the Ardennes towards Antwerp. Although the offensive gave the Allies an unpleasant shock, in the end it was easily repulsed, and the Germans lost all their reserves.

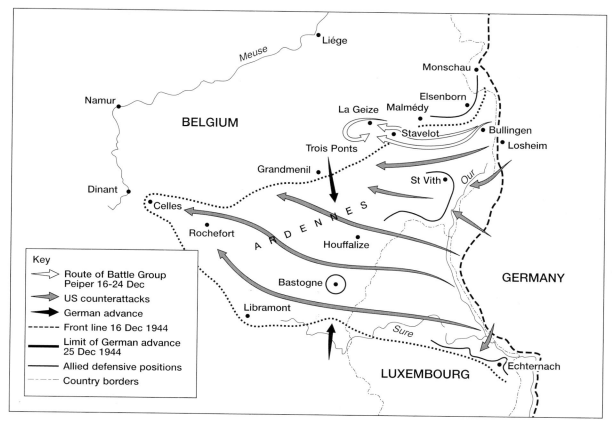

On 22 December, amid a thick curtain of snow and falling temperatures, there was a powerful attack by 1st SS Panzer Grenadier Regiment against the airborne forces at La Gleize. The Cheneux bridgehead was reduced and was ultimately destroyed with an attack across sodden ground by airborne infantry. However, German resistance stiffened as they held on stubbornly to La Gleize and any attempts to dislodge them were seen off with heavy losses. Some consolation to Peiper was the dropping of ammunition and fuel, although the amounts were barely adequate. On the same day, an attack on La Gleize reduced the village to rubble and Peiper, crouching in his cellar headquarters and conscious of the heavy casualties among his men, had to endure increasing isolation and – because of his unreliable ultra high-frequency radio – poor communication. At long last came the permission to break out, but under the condition that vehicles and the wounded accompanied him and his men. With or without vehicles and the wounded, Peiper was determined to move.

The situation steadily worsened: the *Leibstandarte* bridgehead on the Amblève's north bank was being pressurised in the area of Stavelot, to be followed by the capture of much of the Reconnaissance Company on the Trois Ponts road. Of the village Peiper had left behind, Lucas and Cooper record: 'The La Gleize rearguard of 50 men fought to the death. In the woods north of the village other Grenadiers, part of the force which had tried to break through to Peiper, were attacked by infantry of the American 117th and 120th Regiments. Fierce and bitter fighting took place in the dense and snowy woods until the last of these isolated groups of SS men were destroyed.'

The break-out column passed the highway which paralleled the Salm River south of Trois Ponts, and paused to attend their wounded. The only way across was to wade or swim. The weakest were snatched away by the current and perished downstream. Those who made it to the village of Wanne were greeted by US artillery fire, while survivors – some 800 out of an original 1800 – crawled to the refuge of village outhouses. Figures differ as to the exact material losses; however, if those of Cheneux, La Gleize, Stoumont and Stoumont station are added together, the likely tally was 60 tanks, including seven Tigers and 70 half-tracks, as well as flak-weapon assault guns and 105mm (4.13in) and 150mm (5.9in) self-propelled howitzers, together with an incalculable number of trucks and smaller vehicles.

The withdrawal brought the curtain down on the role of 6th Panzer Army in the Ardennes offensive. Manteuffel's 5th Panzer Army could claim better progress with elements of 2nd Panzer Division having driven within a few miles of the Meuse near Dinant. The *Schwerpunkt* (key thrust) of the offensive was therefore transferred to Manteuffel's sector, which meant that Sepp Dietrich was obliged to give up 12th SS Panzer Division *Hitler Jugend* and elements of 1st SS Panzer Division *Leibstandarte* to 5th Panzer Army by 26 December. The survivors among Peiper's men remained within 6th Panzer Army while efforts were made to re-equip them as an armoured reserve.

TURNING POINT

The crucial turning point in the Ardennes theatre had occurred when several divisions of the 3rd Army of General George S. Patton moved up from the south, their main objective being to relieve the key market town of Bastogne, situated on a level plateau surrounded by wooded hills. If the town had been captured, there had been a real danger that German forces would have been much freer to attack the defenders at St Vith and reach the Meuse virtually unopposed. But it was the old story: the Germans totally lacked the resources to capture the town.

On 8 January, Model, whose armies were in danger of entrapment at Houffalize, north-east of Bastogne, finally received permission to withdraw. Precisely a month after the start of the Ardennes campaign, at the cost of some 120,000 casualties and missing, the Germans were literally back to square one. Sepp Dietrich, possibly for the first time in the presence of a senior Nazi, dared voice his disillusion with Hitler. He confided to the Armaments Minister Albert Speer that, in decreeing that Bastogne should be taken at any cost, Hitler had refused to understand that even

Above: This German Panther tank, converted to resemble a US M-10 tank destroyer – complete with star painted on its side and numbers in the front – was intended to confuse and deceive US forces during the offensive.

the SS elite divisions could not effortlessly overrun the Americans. It had been impossible to convince Hitler that these had been tough opponents, soldiers who were as good as his own men.

To Guderian, Chief of the Army General Staff and Commander of the Eastern Front, the folly and dangers of Hitler's exercise were only too clear. He put it succinctly: 'A sensible commander would on this day have remembered the looming dangers on the Eastern Front which could only be countered by a timely breaking off of the operation in the west that was already, from the long view, a failure.'

Guderian sought an interview with Hitler, but the Führer completely lost his temper, shouting and rav-

ing at any attempts to demonstrate the precarious German position on the eve of an expected renewal of the Soviet forces in the north.

However, this display of anger did not come as an undue surprise to Guderian, the acting chief of staff. He had already presented the view of his staff that the Soviets would renew their attack on 12 January with a total superiority of 15 to one. These figures were based on what was then the current German strength on the Eastern Front. Guderian had spent some time pleading with the Führer for the release of troops from the Ardennes and from the Upper Rhine.

But the body blow was yet to come. Hitler overruled Guderian's pleas, furthermore announcing that from then on, the Eastern Front must take care of itself. The Führer was caught up in the grip of a new obsession. It was Hungary – or more specifically, the capital Budapest – which was, by that point, Hitler's latest fixation, and not the Oder.

CHAPTER TEN

LAST THROW

In an attempt to save his last remaining source of oil, Hitler launched
Operation Spring Awakening in Hungary. However, even the
Leibstandarte could not save the day. While they were forced back to
Vienna, Hitler's last stand took place in Berlin.

itler's concentration on Hungary, if viewed separately from his pursuit of an ever-receding dream of ultimate victory, was very practical. The greater part of the Reich's synthetic oil plants lay in ruins from Allied bombing; the wells of Zisterdorf in Austria and those around Lake Balaton in Hungary would be desirable acquisitions. Even Guderian, as one of Hitler's severest critics, had to concede that these were of vital importance to all armed forces. Marshal Rodion Malinovsky and his 2nd Ukrainian Front had driven the Germans out of most of eastern Hungary, but additional forces of Germany's 6th Army were holding out in Budapest. The VI SS Panzer Corps, commanded by *SS-Obergruppenführer* Herbert Gille, had been sent in to relieve the garrison, but failed. The latest proposal was that 6th SS Panzer Army, under Sepp Dietrich, withdraw from the Ardennes to do the job. Not least of the several drawbacks to this plan was the certainty that Allied intelligence would seize upon the absence of 6th SS Panzer Army from their centre of interests and draw accurate conclusions, but Hitler was beyond reason.

Left: A German soldier lies dead on the steps of the Berlin Reichschancellery after the battle for Berlin. Members of the *Leibstandarte* fought in their originally-intended role as Hitler's bodyguard during his last days.

The transfer of the army took place in 290 trains making for Komorn, east of Bratislava. It was inevitably slow, due to conditions which had become only too familiar to Dietrich: heavy snows, fuel shortages and Allied air attacks. But 'Spring Awakening', as the enterprise was named, was by way of being a morale booster. Care was taken to make it appear that keen, well-uniformed and splendidly equipped men were on their way to achieve victory after all. Such new tanks and guns as could be mustered formed the long columns. But it was all cosmetic: replacements and the provision of new vehicles were way beneath what were required. Equipment needs could not be fulfilled, either – a major impediment, since Budapest had fallen to the Soviets in the bleak winter of late February 1945.

NEW COMMANDER

As new commander of the *Leibstandarte*, Dietrich had *SS-Brigadeführer* Otto Kumm, who had previously seen service with SS Panzer Grenadier Division *Wiking* and 7th SS Volunteer Mountain Division *Prince Eugen*. His immediate predecessor, Wilhelm Mohnke, was despatched to Berlin for the defence of the Reich capital. Spring Awakening's aim was to destroy Tolbukhin's 3rd Ukrainian Front and establish a barrier east of the oilfields.

Intelligence at Stavka, the Soviet headquarters, was soon aware that 31 divisions, 11 of them panzer, were assembled with reinforcements. This gave an overall German strength of more than 43,000 officers and men for the attack.

At the start of March, Dietrich assembled 6th Panzer Army between lakes Balaton and Velencze. This, by far the largest force, had at first the cover designation 'Higher Engineer Leader, Army Group South'. The respective commands of 1st and 2nd Panzer Corps remained intact from the Ardennes, with *Leibstandarte* and *Hitler Jugend* as part of 1st Panzer. The 6th Panzer Army was provided with the extra muscle of two cavalry divisions and IV SS Panzer Corps, comprising *Wiking* and *Totenkopf*, as well as an Hungarian infantry division.

The main attack was to be on 6 March 1945, with 6th Army, under the command of Lieutenant General Hermann Balck on the left, and Dietrich on the right. There would then follow subsidiary attacks by Army Group E across the Drava, lying to the south, while 2nd Panzer Army would target to the south of Lake Balaton. The offensive was preceded by a short 30-minute artillery bombardment, but without air support. Dietrich later related: 'The emplacements along the western bank of the Danube … The hard strong enemy, and the marshy terrain, impassable for tanks, prevented our advancing and attaining our goal … When tanks attempted to exploit initial successes, the terrain which was supposed to be frozen hard was found to be wet and marshy.'

This was not the only problem. Colonel Wernke, a *Wehrmacht* general staff officer attached to 6th SS Panzer Army under Dietrich and responsible for its logistic support, later stated: 'We had few reserves and a major lack of ammunition. We had shells but insufficient cartridges for the artillery because the production plants and reserves were in northern Germany. All logistic support channels were broken by the Allied advance. Also there were few motor convoys available.' The Soviets, observing the inability of reserves to make much impression, moved in for the kill. The impossible nature of the terrain meant retaliation was out of the question and Dietrich twice

Right: German soldiers involved in the defence of Hungary in early 1945. Hitler was keen to keep control of Hungarian oil, and so plans were made for a new offensive to relieve Budapest and secure the precious fuel.

requested permission to close down; predictably, each request met with blank refusal.

Earlier there had been bitter fighting at the towns of Azora and Simontornya. The latter, to the east of Lake Balaton, had been secured by the Germans and a bridgehead established across the Sio canal. Such gains were set at naught, as the Russians threw in everything they had and the fighting reached fresh ferocity. The SS inched westwards between the 150km (93 miles) of front between the Danube and Lake Balaton.

HITLER BALLISTIC

The Soviets' intention was to cut off both German armies; 6th Panzer Army was forced to withdraw southwestwards along the lake shore. Hitler's reaction when hearing of this was ballistic. At a situation conference on 23 March, he declared: 'I now demand one thing: the *Leibstandarte*, moreover the entire 6th Panzer Army, be sent the last man available anywhere. I mean immediately! Sepp Dietrich must be informed instantly. Immediately!' And, amid a storm of childishness: 'If we lose the war, it will be Dietrich's fault.'

In the eyes of Hitler, to whom the *Leibstandarte* had always been special, Dietrich had committed the twin heinous sins of disobedience and retreat. For Dietrich, the defeat came hard, not least because it spelt the death of the old spirit of the *Leibstandarte*, long adulterated by the low calibre of intake into the division. Neither he nor any of his colleagues could stem plunging morale: units had begun to withdraw without orders and no one had the power to prevent them.

The final humiliation was the signal sent from Headquarters to 6th SS Panzer Army from Hitler, who was so enraged that he hit out at the most obvious target: 'The Führer believes that the troops have not fought as the situation demanded and orders that

Right: Panzer officers from the 6th SS Panzer Army planning their attack during the final German offensive in the east. By the time the forces reached the start point for the attack, Budapest had already fallen.

the SS divisions *Adolf Hitler*, *Das Reich*, *Totenkopf* and *Hohenstaufen* be stripped of their armbands.' Here Hitler was referring to the insignia carrying the names of the divisions. The actual order to remove the bands was meaningless, since all armbands of ground troops had already been relinquished on their arrival in Hungary as part of the camouflaging of 6th Panzer Army.

To underline the point further, Dietrich's biographer, Charles Messenger, states: 'Sepp himself almost certainly removed his own armband, which was distinctive, as was the remainder of his insignia, being in gold rather than the silver worn by all other *Waffen-SS* members, and was a special distinction which had been conferred on him by Hitler.' As a further security measure, armbands were not worn on uniforms that had been replacements for original ones.

DIETRICH'S REACTION

What happened following Hitler's order has been the subject of differing and contradictory accounts over the years. Dietrich's immediate reaction appears to have been typical of his character and there is no reason to doubt his account of it. He told his Canadian interrogator, Milton Shulman, that he first got excessively drunk and then slept for three hours. His next action was to summon four divisional commanders and throw the signal on the table, saying: 'That's your reward for all you've done over the past five years.'

Some accounts have stated that, in the absence of a blistering reply to a message he had sent to Hitler, Dietrich's next action was to send back all his decorations. This account, however, was erroneous, as is a widely quoted claim that the officers of the *Leibstandarte* tore off their decorations, stuffed them in a chamber pot and sent them to Hitler, along with a human arm with a *Leibstandarte* armband attached. This has all the hallmarks of wishful thinking. The

Above: Men of the *Leibstandarte* cautiously advance towards contact with the enemy. By this stage of the war, all the *Leibstandarte* could do was delay the inevitable, with the Allies advancing on all fronts.

true fate of Dietrich's decorations has been revealed by Charles Messenger, who, during the course of research into Sepp's life, interviewed his family and learnt that a number of the decorations, including the Knight's Cross with Oak Leaves, remain in the possession of Dietrich's eldest son, Wolf-Dieter.

Rumours aside, after sending an initial message, no further action was taken by Hitler in the matter. Neither did Sepp Dietrich pass Hitler's order on to his divisional commanders.

It has also been claimed in some accounts that Hitler intended that stripping the armbands be a purely symbolic action, only a temporary measure. The general postwar consensus among *Leibstandarte* men was that the move was an expression of Hitler's spite, designed to puncture the pride of the once-elite formations. Whatever the motives, the petty action shocked even Himmler, who had been ordered to the front to ensure that the Führer's orders were carried out. The *Reichsführer-SS* remonstrated: 'I would have to drive to the Plattensee [Lake Balaton] to take the crosses off the dead. A German SS man cannot give more than his life to you, my Führer'. It made no difference: the oilfields fell to the Russians on 2 April.

Things were no better elsewhere. The Army Group of General Otto von Wöhler was in danger of being outflanked to the north. Malinovsky thrust towards Bratislava on the Danube in southern Czecho-

Above: Panzer Grenadiers in the last months of the war. The *Leibstandarte* retreated to Vienna, but even a unit of their expertise could not prevent the Red Army taking the city. The division moved west to surrender to US forces.

slovakia, while Marshal Feodor Tolbukhin's 3rd Ukranian Front pushed Wöhler back towards Austria. The latter's failure to counterattack lost him his job. His replacement was General Lothar Rendulic who, in a meeting with Hitler, was told to hold Vienna and prevent the enemy from getting to the Alps or north of the Danube valley.

Within 10 days, 267 tanks were lost as the Soviets carried the advance inexorably towards Austria and the intended capture of Vienna by 2nd and 3rd Ukrainian Fronts. There had already been warning signs: on 16 March, Army Group South had tried to make the Panzer Army serve as a solid wall around Stuhlweissenburg, where the main Soviet thrust was plainly intended as a prelude to the seizure of Vienna. The Austrian capital's defence was to be mainly in the hands of a hastily conscripted Home Guard, the under-trained and sorely equipped *Volkssturm*.

POISONED CHALICE

Dietrich was handed a poisoned chalice: to provide four divisions for the purpose of defending the Austrian capital. He put at the disposal of General von Bünau, Battle Commander of Vienna, 2nd SS Panzer Division and 6th Panzer Division. Both men, as Dietrich was to admit later, had not the least doubt that any defence undertaken by these troops would be possible only for a few days.

Throughout, Dietrich maintained the rough Bavarian humour which had never quite left him. Examples were noted by the former *Hitler Jugend* leader Baldur von Schirach, then in Vienna, who heard Sepp declare: 'We call ourselves 6 Panzer Army because we only have six tanks left.' When Schirach visited Dietrich at his castle command, which was ringed with machine guns, the latter told him: 'I have set up this hedgehog position just in case Adolf wants to wipe me out for not defending Vienna.'

There was not much left to defend. The *Leibstandarte* had been virtually burnt out and 12th SS *Hitler Jugend* Panzer Division severely weakened. Overall manpower stood at 1600 officers and men, and 16 tanks. Lucas and Cooper wrote: 'The Grenadiers were so few in number that a continuous line could not be held. The heavy equipment had not been replaced and petrol shortage threatened to reduce still further the fighting strength. Tank trains were formed to conserve fuel, whereby one or two machines towed a number of others, and by these primitive means sufficient tanks were saved to reform some of the shattered companies.'

The cause was lost. Only Hitler himself remained his inflexible self: Vienna was to be defended to the last man. By 6 April, the Soviets had reached the outskirts of the city and, by the 14th, were at its centre. Dietrich's formations had some kick left, however, and kept up the fight. Their motives were variable: a mixture of steadfast loyalty to Hitler's Bodyguard and an element of sheer bravado.

To this had to be added fear: surrender to the Soviets would have only one outcome. Battered remnants were put into the line to stem the Soviet advance and street fighting was heavy.

Vienna Fallen

It was too late: Red Army tanks rumbled past the area of the wine gardens of Grinzing and other key points

Left: From being the virtual creator of the *Leibstandarte*, Sepp Dietrich, one of the most highly decorated soldiers of Hitler's Third Reich, is photographed by his American captors, preparatory to facing charges as a war criminal.

west and northwest of Vienna. Sheets and pillowcases were hung as tokens of surrender in increasing numbers from windows and doors. Austrians in uniform, both eager to desert but fearful of the Soviets, hid in houses and were given civilian clothing.

Before the arrival of the Russians, the greatest fear for the Germans was the thousands of slave labourers roaming the streets, many of whom had managed to secure weapons. By the evening, Dietrich's chief of staff reported to Army Group South: 'It is the Austrians shooting at us, not Russians.' Dietrich also learnt at this time that Tolbukhin's troops were sweeping through his lines and had virtually encircled the city. The order to hold every foot of ground to the end was disregarded. He ordered his troops to move further west, forming another defence line. Vienna was lost.

Dietrich withdrew his remnants to a line west of Vienna and on to Gloggnitz in the south-east. Seemingly tireless, he invaded such training establishments as he could find and dragged out their reluctant inhabitants to strengthen the line. Soon there was the prospect of facing the US forces racing through southern Germany.

Hitler was now busily playing with phantom armies. He sent *Das Reich* to prop up what was left of Army Group Centre in Czechoslovakia, where the Soviets had moved in to capture the important industrial centre of Brno. The 6th SS Panzer Army and the *Leibstandarte* could do nothing in the face of this but withdraw.

On 7 May, in the French city of Reims, the capitulation of the Wehrmacht was signed. Field Marshal Albert Kesselring, signatory to the document of surrender, sent a message to Dietrich: 'The terms of the ceasefire are also binding on all formations of the SS. I expect that, like the entire *Wehrmacht*, the *Leibstandarte* will also conduct itself in an irreproachably correct manner.' The final message to reach Kesselring read: 'The regiment, cut off from all supplies, down to less than a third of the strength with which it went into Hungary, must now capitulate. Tomorrow we shall march into captivity with heads held high. The regiment that had the once proud honour of bearing the name *Leibstandarte* is now signing off.'

Similar residues of discipline remained at the River Enns, south of Steyr in Austria, on whose west bank the Americans waited for surrendering Germans.

SURRENDER

There was an effort, according to *Twelve Years with Hitler*, an account of *Leibstandarte*'s 1st Company, to present the men 'with steel helmets on, collars buttoned, sitting upright in their vehicles with rifles in hand'. The grand symbolic gesture was firmly eschewed by Dietrich. Accompanied by his wife, Ursula, he surrendered to Master Sergeant Herbert Kraus of US 36 Infantry Division at Kufstein to the south-east of Munich. The American told how he was not in the slightest bit overwhelmed by his prisoner, and that he regarded him as 'not anything like an army commander – he is more like a village grocer'.

Dietrich's surrender could be said to bring the saga of the *Leibstandarte* to a close, but there were those who remained steadfastly on duty until the war's end. In Berlin, Hitler had moved into his underground bunker 16.75m (55ft) below the Reich Chancellery, a sweaty, concrete sarcophagus with its elaborate complex of shelters. The bunker was supplied with a modest switchboard, as well as one radio transmitter and one radio-telephone link with *Wehrmacht* headquarters at Zossen, 24km (15 miles) south of Berlin.

For the Führer, communication with the outside world was restricted to the hours of darkness, when he would occasionally emerge to take his German shepherd dog, Blondi, for a brief walk through the rubbish-strewn paths of the Chancellery garden. At a discreet distance hovered members of the *Leibstandarte*, men who, by fulfilling the old function of ensuring Hitler's safety, had been lucky enough to avoid sharing the death agonies of their comrades in Austria. In addition, other troops numbering several thousand in SS Guard Battalion 1, under Mohnke, defended as best they could the government quarter of Berlin and approaches to the Chancellery. They also fulfilled a far more sinister function. As members

of the *Führerbeglietkommando* (FBK), which it will be recalled had come into being in the early days of Hitler's Chancellorship, they implemented orders given to them by Himmler to set up flying 'courts martial', carrying out instant executions on deserters, who were frequently driven out of Berlin cellars to be left dangling from lamp posts.

Various units forming as battle groups were men of 1st Company of the *Leibstandarte*, marshalling in the area of Berlin-Marienfelde. They were instructed to drive down the Wilhelmstrasse to the Reich Chancellery where, after a relatively quiet period, Soviet artillery fired the first shells. An *SS-Rottenführer* of 1st Company was billeted with his comrades in the vast basements of what had been the Reichsbank, along with young and old Berliners who were seeking shelter:

'There was no panic, and we young soldiers followed all orders, trusting in the strength of the "invincible" fortress Berlin ... Thrown together units made up of soldiers from every arm, combat veterans of the *Waffen-SS*, members of the *Volkssturm* and even sailors, fought against the approaching Red Army.'

STREET FIGHTING

Fighting raged in the streets, with tank fire, mortars and snipers. Mohnke, having torched the by then empty bunker on 1 May 1945 and reportedly said farewell to his Führer amid floods of tears, had fled the city where the newly married Hitler and Eva Braun were to commit suicide. During the night 6/7 May, following the cessation of hostilities by Army Group South, the remnants of the *Leibstandarte* marched southwards towards the US lines.

Not all of them embodied the old spirit of the *Leibstandarte*. The *Waffen-SS* qualities of racial and physical purity originally demanded by Himmler – who was to take poison on his capture by the British – had long since perished. Many of those mustered into the prisoner-of-war cages were the product of sweepings born of desperation: low-calibre recruits, superannuated airmen and sailors, and some factory workers who quaked at so much as a shot from a machine pistol.

Above: The Führer congratulates *Obergruppenführer* **Hermann Fegelein, who had just married Gretl Braun, the sister of Hitler's mistress, Eva. He was shot on Hitler's orders on 29 April 1945 by members of the** *Leibstandarte*.

By contrast, the comrades they left behind in Berlin had kept faith with their Führer until the very end. They included the *Leibstandarte* men who, in the bunker, were responsible for carrying out the ritual execution of *Obergruppenführer* Hermann Fegelein, Himmler's chief liaison man. Fegelein had deserted the bunker and taken refuge in his own home. Hitler became convinced that Fegelein had also turned traitor and that he was in league with Himmler – who, it turned out, had been holding secret negotiations to surrender the German armies in the west to Eisenhower.

This was the last commission that the *Leibstandarte* was able to carry out in defence of their Führer on his home ground. As a militarily effective force, it had long shot its bolt. Gone were the immaculate and uniformed robots who, in the old days, had stood guard, ramrod-straight, at the portals of the Reich Chancellery. The veterans who survived to the end, however, considered that they had kept the faith, their reputation secure in their own eyes and only besmirched by the outside world which had scant sympathy for their pretensions to being an elite unit. In the eyes of a shattered Europe, the men of the *Leibstandarte* were, quite simply, as SS men, members of a criminal band who would face the forces of international justice. Even granting their often sublime courage as fighting men, it was truly an ignoble end for 'Hitler's own'.

CHAPTER ELEVEN

KEY FIGURES

The *Leibstandarte* was essentially Adolf Hitler's creation, but its chief gladiator and driving force was Sepp Dietrich. As well as its star tankmen, there were others who performed key roles in the development and performance of the division.

When Sepp Dietrich was born on 28 May 1892 to Palagius and Kreszentia Dietrich, in the small village of Hawangen near Memmingen in Swabia, the old Hohenzollern empire still had a quarter of a century left to run. Many of those who had served it – senior military figures such as von Manstein, the son of an artillery officer, and von Rundstedt, the aristocratic Brandenburger and military academy graduate – had come from very different backgrounds from the Dietrichs. A respectable member of the Roman Catholic working class, Sepp's father Palagius earned his living as a *Packermeister* (master packer), and Dietrich's first experiences of working life were in the role of a baker's boy (and not, incidentally, as many biographies would assert, as a butcher) as well as an agricultural driver.

INAUSPICIOUS START

The start of his army career was inauspicious. His month with the 4th Field Artillery Regiment, which he joined at Augsburg in October 1911, ended when

Left: On the completion of living quarters for himself and a deputy at Lichterfelde barracks, Sepp Dietrich celebrates in the mess. Typically of him, invitations were also extended to those who were involved in the building work.

he fell from a horse and was invalided out. As his biographer Charles Messenger reveals, when Dietrich was in captivity at the end of World War II, he drew up a record of his early military career that was scarcely accurate. He claimed, for example, that he had served in the cavalry, rather than serving in the infantry, a unit which did not carry the same social prestige as the cavalry. Neither was the additional claim that he had gone on to become an *Unteroffizier* (NCO) for mountain troops true. Many of the contradictions and inconsistencies about his service at this period eventually were to find their way into his SS file. Other claims Dietrich made cannot be confirmed one way or the other, mainly through lack of documentation.

One theory often advanced to account for some of his elaboration was that, since he was naturally ambitious, he was seeking to present the best account of himself when it came to preparing for a career. What can be established is that, on 6 August 1914, caught up in the patriotic fervour of the time, Sepp Dietrich enlisted in the 7th Bavarian Field Artillery Regiment, which came under the 6th Army of Crown Prince Rupprecht of Bavaria. Dietrich's introduction to action would have been immediate, since the 6th Army was in the front line from the moment it reached Flanders. Wounded

Right: Dietrich, and on his left Carl Auen of the State Film Organisation, help collect money for *Winterhilfswerk*, a relief organisation supplying clothes, fuel and food for the needy, on Berlin's Unter den Linden in January 1935.

more than once, he received shrapnel wounds in the right leg and, despite the near demise of cavalry by that time, suffered a lance thrust above the left eye. The latter wound was received during the combat at the Ypres front.

In February 1918, Dietrich received a new posting with Bavarian Storm Tank Detachment 13. It was during this period that there was a happening which was quintessential Sepp and which, incidentally, won him the Bavarian Military Merit Cross. Moritz, one of the Detachment's Mark IV tanks in action near Rheims, had acquitted itself well against the French front line with its six-pounder and machine guns. Moritz then sunk into a shell hole and efforts to get it out again resulted only in an overheated engine. Demolition of the armoured vehicle was the only answer. Consequently Dietrich was mustered along with two others for the demolition party. Assailed by heavy fire, with Moritz steadily being reduced to scrap iron, Dietrich dived into the steaming hulk to rescue a bottle of schnapps which he knew was lurking in there. It was a coup that made him a legend and which also did no harm at all to Moritz's first driver, Maier, whom Dietrich later encountered in Munich. In recognition of former days, Dietrich was instrumental in elevating his old colleague to *SS-Standartenführer* rank.

DISCHARGED

Dietrich was discharged on 26 March 1918 from 7th Bavarian Field Artillery Regiment with the rank of *Wachtmeister* (sergeant major) and the Iron Cross, II Class. Returning to Bavaria in November 1918, he had hoped for a position in the postwar army, but there was scant sympathy for veterans at that time. Instead, the main concern of the authorities was striving to control the anarchy and violence committed by various political groups erupting in the former kingdom, not least coming from hard-line nationalists,

Left: During January 1941, Sepp Dietrich and the *Leibstandarte* play host to General Oberst Johannes von Blaskowitz, who commanded an army in the invasion of Poland and over the next two years would do so in Russia.

including the fledgling National Socialists. The best option for the former sergeant major was with the green uniformed paramilitary *Landpolizei*, which he joined, it is believed, in the early 1920s. The *Landpolizei* was organised on infantry division lines and was looking not for permanent members, but for a pool of reserves in the event of national emergency. The creation of such paramilitary police was a handy way of circumventing the rigid 100,000-man army restriction which had been imposed by the Treaty of Versailles in 1919; here in the *Landpolizei*, many fondly hoped, was the foundation for tomorrow's Bavarian Army.

MEETING WITH HITLER

The precise date of Dietrich's parting from the *Landpolizei* cannot be established. What is known is that he took a number of jobs in quick succession: clerk for a tobacco company and a job with the customs services, as well as the more humble type of employment in a filling station. However, it was the last which was to prove the most significant, as a meeting there sowed the seeds for his future SS career. The garage manager was Christian Weber, whom, as we have seen, was one of Hitler's earliest followers. By the summer of 1921, Hitler had gained the leadership of the NSDAP, and it was around this time that he and Dietrich met.

At this point, however, Dietrich was still beholden to the *Landpolizei* and so he made no immediate attempt then to pursue the contact. His baptism of fire in politics ran parallel with his quitting the *Landespolizei* and becoming a member of the *Freikorps* (Free Corps) *Oberlander*, one of the many armed bands springing up all over Germany. These were financed, secretly trained and also equipped by the *Reichswehr* (which was the basis of the future *Wehrmacht*). In William Shirer's words, these bands consisted of 'the great mob of demobilised soldiers for whom the bottom had fallen out of the world in 1918, uprooted men who could not find jobs or their way back to the peaceful society they had left in 1914, men grown tough and violent through war who could not shake themselves from ingrained habit …' These men were all united in a common bond: that is, they harboured a contempt for the democratic republic which had been established in Berlin.

The *Freikorps* might have been made for Dietrich. Early in his membership of *Freikorps Oberlander*, he was involved in the fight against the incursions of Polish nationalists laying claim to the rich industrial

region of Upper Silesia. An observer of that time recalled seeing him arriving in Silesia with fellow Oberlanders, dressed in 'ruffians' clothes' and showing 'enormous military knowledge and both bravery and initiative in the face of the enemy'. Whether or not Dietrich played any significant part in the farcical Beer Hall Putsch of 8/9 November 1923 is not known precisely, although he may well have done as a *Friekorps* platoon leader, thus facing dismissal for implicitly siding with Hitler in the bid to overthrow the government.

It was not until May 1928 that the NSDAP gained its first real opportunity in the political arena with the election of deputies to the Reichstag. The result was disappointing – only 12 out 491 seats were secured – but it was a start. In that year, Dietrich became an NSDAP member. As Party Member No.

Below: Sepp Dietrich greets one of his officers at Olchowatke during a tour of inspection in the winter of 1942/3. Dietrich is wearing a sheepskin jacket to protect against the Russian cold.

89015 of the NSDAP – which, incidentally, was to entitle him to the Gold Party badge as one of the first 100,000 members – his future became solidly assured. He was not slow to make his mark as a member of the *Schutzstaffel* (SS), becoming *Sturmführer* on 1 June 1928 and, that same year, entering SS *Sturm* 1 (SS Battalion 1) with the number 1177, rising to command the Munich SS detachment or *Standarte*. By May of the following year, he had assumed command of SS Brigade *Bayern*, embracing the entire SS in Bavaria.

Shortly after all this, he became one of Hitler's personal bodyguards. The state of the party's finances was such that he could not be paid and he had to provide his own black uniform – a plight remedied when he joined the Nazi publishing firm of Eber-Verlag as a clerk. It was a lowly job, compensated for when, in the September 1930 election, Dietrich was voted on the NSDAP ticket into the Reichstag for the constituency of Upper Bavaria-Swabia. Here, he adopted no overt political stance, but was useful voting fodder for the National Socialist lobby.

Dietrich was not simply called upon to provide muscle and fisticuffs as Hitler's bodyguard, although there were occasions when both were required. It meant being a member of the tightest group of confidantes around the Führer, men whom he could trust completely. The former *Gefreiter* (lance corporal) and the former sergeant major had taken to each other instantly, a rapport that accounted for the Führer's oft-repeated remark: 'Dietrich is one of my oldest companions in the struggle.' An indication of how highly he was regarded can be seen in the fact that he was one of the very few men at this time ever to be granted a private audience with his Führer. It was perhaps inevitable that Dietrich was the man to whom Hitler turned when it came to setting up the *Leibstandarte*, an assignment that brought promotion to *SS-Obergruppenführer*.

CHARISMA

No photograph was able to do justice to Dietrich's abundant charisma, a quality commented on by General Heinrich Eberbach, Inspector of Panzer Troops at Normandy, who said of him: 'Sepp Dietrich is something grand.' In appearance, he was small with a ballooning belly which signified a strong liking for beer, but he deferred to no one when it came to holding his liquor. The Canadian Milton Shulman wrote of a man 'short and squat with a broad dark face, dominated by a large white nose', resembling 'a rather battered bartender. He was a typical product of the Free Corps and the bullying gang with which Hitler first made his advent on the political stage.' His conversational approach was rough and ready, salted with Bavarian oaths and a humour described by a subordinate as 'always coarse, often vulgar and sometimes foul'.

Dietrich's attitude to his men, one of his greatest strengths, can be illustrated by two incidents, the first vividly expressed by one of his former SS officers: 'Sepp is all things to us. First and foremost he is a leader, of that there can be no doubt – one of the best …. He is a father figure. He has never lost his NCO attitude to his men. For example when presenting medals other generals walk up and down the ranks with a solemnity that would do justice to a pall-bearer. Not so Dietrich. He looks at the men as if he knows them personally, adjusts a cap, pushes in a stomach, comments on this and that, and generally acts in a way that tells us that we are individual men not just numbers …

'He can be hard on us, but seemingly never without justification. The other day he saw a patrol that had just come off duty, the men tired dirty and hungry. One man, however, had slung his rifle in a manner Dietrich cannot abide. That was that. Dietrich had that man doing press-up, sit-ups, the lot, for over half an hour and he supervised it all. After it was over the man looked half-dead and Dietrich sent him on his way with a bar of chocolate!'

The other example, told in the journal *Der Freiwillige* (*The Volunteer*), recalls the time when the *Leibstandarte* was withdrawn into reserve in the area of the port of Mariupol on the Sea of Azov. It was a quiet period and as such was enjoyed by the 37mm (1.45in) flak-gun crews. Food, however, was in short supply and the men had put a sign outside their quarters reading 'Hunger Tavern'. Soviet aircraft flew over, but often at too low a height for the flak guns to make hits. Then there was a visit from Sepp Dietrich:

'He emanates a calmness which is felt by his soldiers and which is carried over to them. When he sees the sign he wants to know its purpose. Then he goes to the gun; he wants to know how it is operated. He takes the gunlayer's seat and moves the gun up and down. He asks whether he can fire it ... They ... tell him of the Russian planes which regularly fly over. Before he leaves, he gives them a packet of cigarettes. He orders them to send two men to Divisional HQ. To the gun commander he says that during World War One he had always taken care that his men had had something to eat, to keep morale high. When the two men came back from Divisional HQ they could hardly carry the food. They changed the sign to "Flax Recreation Centre". And, really, Dietrich comes back the following day to have a go with the gun. But he misses as well.'

FATHER FIGURE

As for Dietrich's prowess as a soldier, the pronouncement by the official SS journal, *Das Schwarze Korps (The Black Corps)*, was as might be expected, complimentary. Here, it proclaimed, was 'the father of his men ... the model for his unit commanders, a hard soldier with a strange tender heart for his comrades. Ruthless in combat, demanding the ultimate in attack ... a knight without heart and without reproach: the National Socialist soldier'.

To Hermann Göring, Sepp Dietrich was 'the pillar of the Eastern Front'. But there is also von Rundstedt's condemnation of Dietrich as 'decent but stupid' and the oft-quoted incident from Felix Steiner: 'I once spent an hour and a half trying to explain a situation to Sepp Dietrich with the aid of a map. It was quite useless. He understood nothing at all.' To that can be added Paul Hausser's snap judgment: 'Ordinarily, he would make a fair sergeant major, a better sergeant and a first-class corporal.' To Milton Shulman, he appeared crude, conceited and garrulous, a man whose 'meteoric career was

undoubtedly achieved more by his hard and ruthless energy than by his military ability'.

The judgment of his principal staff officer, Rudolf Lehmann, on the eve of the battle of Kursk, seems fairer: '... he was no strategic genius but a leader of the highest quality of soldiers and of men. He could not use this gift as a commanding general nor as the commander in chief of an army; it suffered a lot because of this. Neither was it his strength to formulate perfect tactical judgments on a situation. But he possessed a special sense for

what would become crisis points, especially how to develop them favourably.'

Whatever is the true verdict, Sepp Dietrich emerged from the war as one of the most highly decorated commanders of the German armed forces. His Knight's Cross was awarded on 7 July 1940, followed by his Oak Leaves (31 December 1941), the Swords (16 March 1943) and finally the Diamonds to the Knight's Cross on 6 August 1944. The value that Hitler attached to Dietrich can be measured in the knowledge that only 27 'Diamonds' were awarded. In

Above: Dietrich with Fritz Witt at Kharkov in 1943. Witt was one of the original members of the *Leibstandarte*, and was killed in Normandy on 16 June 1944 while leading the *Hitler Jugend* Division. His replacement was Kurt Meyer.

addition, Dietrich was further promoted to the rank of *Oberstgruppenführer* on 1 August 1944 and received the full title of *Oberstgruppenführer und Panzergeneral-Oberst der Waffen-SS.*

With his surrender to US forces and the cessation of his career, Dietrich faced a period of ten and

a half years imprisonment. On 16 April 1946, he was formally arrested and charged by the United States Counter-Intelligence Corps (CIC). In the following month, he lost his prisoner of war status, facing trial with 73 others, including Joachim Peiper, primarily for participation in the massacre at the Baugnez crossroads near Malmédy, but also for killings at some dozen other locations in Belgium between 16 December 1944 and 13 January 1945. Dietrich was sentenced to 25 years imprisonment, but there were claims that in order to placate naturally indignant public opinion, witnesses had been harassed into giving false admissions and there had been insufficient evidence of direct participation by some of the accused. Consequently, Dietrich was paroled after serving nine years of his sentence. He was, however, given a further 18-month custodial sentence by a German court, to be served again at Landsberg, for his part in the killing of the SA leaders during the summer of 1934 in the so-called Night of the Long Knives.

By any measure, it was an incomprehensibly lenient punishment. Under his direction during the purge, the *Leibstandarte* had become nothing more than a killing machine. As well as the original shootings of six prominent SA leaders at Stadelheim Prison, Dietrich had deputed *Sturmbannführer* Martin Kohlroser to form execution squads. According to later figures, the bodies of 14 hitherto close comrades alleged to have been involved in a coup against Himmler were soon being heaped like rotting vegetables against the walls of Lichterfelde barracks.

On release from his prison sentences, Sepp Dietrich devoted himself to membership, of necessity largely passive, of the postwar *Hilfsorganisation auf Gegenseitigkeit der Waffen-SS* (SS-HIAG, or Waffen Self-Help Organisation), which within a few years gained a certain respectability and was even allowed to advertise. However, his health – notably growing circulatory prob-

Left: Dietrich was always a law unto himself. Here, wearing a lighter-coloured uniform than his fellow commanders, he meets Colonel-General Hoth, commander of the 4th Panzer Army at the battle for Kursk.

lems and a serious heart condition – began to decline. He died of a massive heart attack on 21 April 1966. At his funeral, former comrades bore the coffin, which was draped with the flag of the Iron Cross with a helmet and sword resting upon it, to the grave at Ludwigsburg.

One of the last public sightings of Sepp Dietrich not long before his death is worth recalling. Dietrich had stood with sightseers to watch a procession of his former comrades, but did not himself take part. A reporter noticed the squat figure in the crowd and approached Dietrich for his reaction. He shrugged with a wan smile, 'Let them have their fun.'

JOACHIM ('JOCHEN') PEIPER

Even though his death took place 31 years after the war's end, Joachim ('Jochen') Peiper is regarded by the dwindling number of *Leibstandarte* survivors as the last German soldier to have been a *Gefallene* (casualty) of World War II. As one of his biographers, British Major General Michael Reynolds, points out, the leader of *Kampfgruppe* (Combat Group) *Peiper* 'died in similar circumstances to those in which he found himself so many times in the war – in a "cauldron" surrounded by enemies'. There, however, any resemblance to a soldier's death ends.

The legend of the courage of Jochen Peiper remains, inevitably darkened by the stain of brutality which attaches to his unit. He was born in Berlin on 30 January 1915 to Woldemar and Charlotte Peiper. His father had served in World War I and subsequently worked in the lottery business. His son – there were three brothers in all – left Berlin's Goethe Oberrealschule with an unremarkable scholastic record. He entered the *Leibstandarte* as SS No. 132496 in 1934 and was selected for training at the SS Junkerschule Braunschweig. As a potential member of Hitler's Bodyguard, he had sworn allegiance to his Führer in the torchlight ceremony in front of the Feldherrnhalle War Memorial in Munich. After a spell of duty with his unit, he became Adjutant to *Reichsführer-SS* Heinrich Himmler, an ideal stepping stone for an SS career.

It has been the constantly reiterated claim of *Waffen-SS* apologists that members of the *Leibstandarte* were primarily soldiers like any other. However, as Michael Reynolds points out: 'As personal Adjutant he would have been privy to virtually everything in Himmler's office and he could not have failed to be aware of Hitler's and Himmler's policies for the ethnic cleansing of the Greater Reich, the organisation and establishment of concentration camps and the overall policy for the genocide of the Jewish race.' Indeed, it is undeniable that Peiper possessed both the ideological convictions of a proclaimed National Socialist and the characteristic arrogance of the *Waffen-SS* man. But there was general agreement among *Leibstandarte* survivors that, in many ways, he was not a typical product of the SS.

Unlike many of his compatriots, he was intelligent, humorous and well read with a serviceable command of English and French. When he had undergone examination prior to training at the cadet school, the doctors had considered him somewhat small for the SS and not as well built as most of the candidates. Furthermore, as to his personality, it was found that he possessed 'strong will and inclined to realise that will in quick impulsive thrusts'.

COMPANY COMMANDER

At the outbreak of war, Peiper was a company commander earning an impressive record in Poland and France, receiving the Iron Cross, both classes. After able service in Greece and Russia, he was promoted to *SS-Sturmbannführer* in mid-1942 and appointed to command the 3rd Battalion of the 2nd SS Panzer Regiment. Early in April of the next year he received the Knight's Cross and, the following November, rose to command the 1st SS Panzer Regiment with the rank of *SS-Obersturmbannführer*. He received the Oak Leaves on 21 January 1944 and finally the Swords in December.

Any consideration of Peiper's record in the Ardennes offensive has to take account both of his combat expertise and that of his Panzer Group, and a record of mass murder. Seventy-one members of Combat Group *Peiper* and three generals of 6th Panzer Army were arraigned before a US Military Court at Dachau on 16 May 1946, charged with crimes 'at or in

the vicinity of Malmédy'. The proceedings had been arranged hurriedly and under pressure from American public opinion, in the face of almost daily revelations about the depths of Nazi brutality, the crimes alleged against the *Leibstandarte* included. Before a court of six US officers came the accusations of war crimes. Forty-three of the defendants, including Peiper, were sentenced to death by hanging.

At no time during their confinement in the fortress of Landsberg were Peiper and the others allowed to forget the fate which awaited them; they were made to wear tracksuit tops coloured red to signify that the gallows was their destination. Not the least controversial aspect of the trial had been the reliance on confessions by the accused, since no direct evidence of who had been responsible for the shootings was available. Even the guilt of Fleps, the man alleged to have been the first to open fire on the Americans and who had been sentenced to death, could not be established conclusively, since it seemed clearly impossible for any German to be identified with certainty within a few seconds of the shooting commencing. There were also allegations that prisoners had been deprived of food, beaten frequently and subjected to kangaroo courts while in custody. The death sentences which had been handed down were eventually commuted.

Peiper was released on parole on 22 December 1956. Nearly five years had been spent in solitary confinement wearing the 'red top' and a total eleven and a half years had gone by while Peiper was a prisoner. In his book *The Devil's Adjutant*, Michael Reynolds quotes from a 1967 interview that Peiper gave to a French writer. The words reported by the writer showed the extent to which Peiper remained unrepentant: 'I was a Nazi and I remain one ... The Germany of today is no longer a great nation, it has become a province of Europe. That is why, at the first opportunity, I shall settle elsewhere, in France no doubt. I don't particularly care for Frenchmen, but I love France. Of all things, the materialism of my compatriots causes me pain.'

In 1972, after jobs first as a clerk with the Porsche Motor Company, and then as a publishing executive

post ceased, Peiper and his wife Sigi could no longer afford their home in Stuttgart. The couple moved to a modest chalet-type home near the small village of Traves in eastern France. Here, Peiper undertook book translation work. It was a peaceful existence until his identity was unmasked and he began receiving a series of death threats, followed by a carefully orchestrated hate campaign. This included the daubing of swastikas and SS runes in and around Traves. In the early hours of 14 July 1976, when Peiper was sleeping alone in the house, a neighbour was woken by the sound of the village siren and saw flames engulfing Peiper's house. Beneath his barely recognisable body lay a .22 calibre rifle. The remains of three Molotov cocktails were also found.

The file relating to Peiper's death is held by the Police Judiciare in Dijon. Over the years, allegations

Above: Sepp Dietrich, revered by his men with whom he cultivated an instant rapport, and who is remembered fondly today by the declining number of *Leibstandarte* veterans. To others, he had a darker side.

have been made that the authorities were protecting survivors of the French Resistance from prosecution, while other ascribed the murder to French communists, particularly as, a month before the fire, the left-wing newspaper *L'Humanite* had printed an article 'exposing' Peiper. Whatever the truth, the murder of Himmler's one-time adjutant was never solved.

MICHAEL WITTMANN

For farmer's son Michael Wittmann, considered by many the foremost tank commander of World War II, a career in the *Leibstandarte* was a quantum leap

Above: Former *Waffen-SS* commanders on trial in Dachau as war criminals before a military court on 16 May 1946. Pictured on the front row, left to right, are: Sepp Dietrich, Fritz Kramer, Hermann Priess and Joachim Peiper.

indeed. Born in the small village of Vogethal near Beilgries in the Oberpfalz region of Bavaria, he might well have spent his life working on the land with the rest of his family. Instead, he opted for the army. Like so many of his generation, he was optimistic about 'the new Germany', which he was convinced heralded good times – above all, in a rejuvenated army free from the intolerable restraints of the Treaty of Versailles.

In 1934, aged 20, he was assigned to 10th Company of the 19th Infantry Regiment, based at Freising near Munich, with whom he remained until October 1936, reaching the rank of *Gefreiter* (lance corporal). Wittmann was attracted first to the *Allgemeine-SS* (General SS), but it was the growing

Waffen-SS that was open to those with talent and he had no trouble in passing the stringent physical requirements. Regarded as a high-flyer, he was talent-spotted to join the *SS-Verfügungstruppe* (*SS-VT*) and was accepted as a recruit with 17 Company of the *Leibstandarte*, going into training at Lichterfelde.

On joining the *Leibstandarte*, Wittmann had become an *SS-Mann*, the SS equivalent of *Gefreiter*. He trained as an army car crewman, with an introduction to a number of small four-wheeled light reconnaissance vehicles, useful for a tank man. By the outbreak of war, Wittmann was an *SS-Unterscharführer* in command of an armoured car in Poland and France, but the real opportunity to show off his skills came when the *Leibstandarte* took delivery of a number of new vehicles, with their Sturmgeschutz III Ausf. A (StuG III) self-propelled assault guns.

While stationed at Metz following the campaign in France, Wittmann begged his commanding officer to let him train on the new vehicles. Later, with his commanding officer's consent, Wittman was to personally select his three-man crew. Training was intense and also highly realistic. As Armoured Fighting Vehicle Crews (AFVs), Wittmann and his colleagues had to become familiar with their tanks in record time and be ready, if necessary, to strip them down in the field. By the latter part of 1940, the stringent StuG training was complete and Wittmann's crew were impatient for action. The call came in April 1941, following Italy's botched invasion of the Balkans and Mussolini's plea for assistance.

GREEK ADVENTURE

While the *Leibstandarte* was in action in Greece during Operation Marita, most of the limelight went to *Obersturmführer* Kurt 'Panzer' Meyer. However, Wittmann and his StuG III crew also played its part in the assault on the heavily fortified Klissura Pass and the resulting push towards Kastoria, with the capture of 12,000 men of the Greek 13th Division. It was during this campaign that Michael Wittmann was awarded the Iron Cross, II Class. With the invasion of the Soviet Union in 1941, he was to be in the thick of the fighting in and around Uman, and his bravery there earned him the Iron Cross, I Class.

In its storm towards the Crimea, the *Leibstandarte* regrouped for a night-time assault on the town of Melitopol. Wittmann confronted two Soviet tank guns, smashing into the vehicles and their crews, who scattered in panic. Despite the attention of Russia's hidden enemy 'General Winter' and the consequent slowing down of the German juggernaut, there had been the successful contribution of the *Leibstandarte*

to the capture of the towns of Stalino and Taganrog, and the city of Rostov.

Wittmann was considered to be officer material and, at the end of 1942, was sent to the SS Junkerschule Bad Toldt and subsequently promoted to *Untersturmführer*. When he rejoined the *Leibstandarte*, he became section commander in the 13th (Heavy) Company of the 1st SS Panzer Regiment. His achievements during the Kursk offensive have often been detailed in accounts of that period; his bold, virtually single-handed attack in the area of Villers-Bocage in Normandy led to his promotion to *SS-Hauptsturmführer* on the endorsement of General Fritz Bayerlein of Panzer *Lehr*, which he had saved from certain destruction. To Wittmann now fell the honour of becoming the most decorated tanker ace of World War II. On 25 June 1944, Adolf Hitler presented him with the Swords for his Knight's Cross with Oak Leaves on the recommendation of Sepp Dietrich.

It was felt that a *Leibstandarte* man of Wittmann's experience could be best employed in the instruction of fledging recruits from the *Waffen-SS* training schools, but Wittman refused to be considered for this role – fatally, as it turned out. Instead, August 1944 found him in the thick of the fighting around Caen, which was facing total destruction in face of the German bid to hold the town.

At that time, Wittmann secured a new Tiger (//007) and was transferred to the area of Cintheaux, where fighting soon broke out. According to a report by a *SS-Hauptscharführer* of Tiger //213, positioned to the rear right of //007 near the road to Caen-Cintheaux at Gaumesnil, Wittmann's tank was destroyed by an explosion which tore its turret away from its hull. The five-man crew was killed.

There were no eyewitnesses or survivors on that fateful day – 8 August 1944 – to describe conclusively what had happened. Claims of the kill have been made by veterans of A Squadron of Britain's Northamptonshire Yeomanry, stating that they opened fire with the 17-pounder gun of a British Sherman VC 'Firefly'. Another theory was that a high-explosive rocket had been fired from a Royal Air

Left: *SS-Obersturmbannführer* Joachim ('Jochen') Peiper, commander of 1st SS Panzer Regiment *Leibstandarte Adolf Hitler* in the Ardennes and Hungary. Peiper had previously served in France, Greece and Russia.

Right: A rare moment of contemplation is afforded these two *Leibstandarte* tank men on the streets of Kharkov in March 1943 after the II SS Panzer Corps' victory. They are Jochen Peiper (left) and Fritz Witt (hands in pockets).

Force Hawker 'Typhoon' MkIB attack aircraft, conspicuous in their attacks on German armour in Normandy. The rocket, so went the claim, hit the 25mm (1in) thick armour of the Tiger's rear deck, causing the engine compartment to explode. A second explosion was said to have set off the tank's store of ammunition, which killed the crew and blew the turret into the air.

After Wittmann failed to return at the end of the day's fighting, a search was made by members of Wittmann's battalion and a party from 12th SS Panzer Division *Hitler Jugend*. The crew of //007 was buried in an unmarked grave next to the stricken Tiger, where the bodies remained until they were discovered during road construction work in March 1983. After identification of Wittmann's remains from surviving dental records and from the identity tag of the Tiger's driver, *SS-Unterscharführer* Henrich Reimers, there was an official burial in the German Military Cemetery of De La Cambe in Normandy.

To his comrades in the *Leibstandarte*, Michael Wittmann was a professional of quiet demeanour who kept his nerve throughout combat and who possessed almost a sixth sense when judging the likely moves of his opponents. This was a gift shared to a large degree by his high-calibre crews, who came to anticipate his likely orders and who gave him full cooperation. In their eyes, Michael Wittmann was the supreme *Leibstandarte* tank hero, fighting for his Fatherland to the very end.

THEODOR WISCH

The first successor to Sepp Dietrich as commander of the *Leibstandarte* – a position he held from 20 August 1944 until 6 February 1945 – 'Teddy' Wisch was born on 13 December 1907 in Wesselburener Hoog. After relinquishing his studies in architecture, he became one of the earliest members of the *Leibstandarte* in March 1933. In the same year, he enjoyed promotion to *SS-Untersturmführer* and, within three months, had attained *SS-Hauptsturmführer*. His prowess as company leader in the Polish campaign brought him both the coveted I and II classes of the Iron Cross. He served in France, Greece and Russia as an *SS-Sturmbannführer*, and was awarded the Knights Cross in September 1941.

In June 1942, Wisch became Commander of the 22nd SS Panzer Grenadier Regiment, and subsequently earned the German Cross in Gold after Kharkov. At 36 years old, as *SS-Brigadeführer und Generalmajor der Waffen-SS*, Wisch was appointed successor to Dietrich on 27 July 1943.

In December of the following year, he was awarded the Oak Leaves, followed by the Swords to his

Knight's Cross. His career, however, was brought to an abrupt end when he was badly wounded during the action in Normandy. As a result of this wound, he was obliged to relinquish command of the *Leibstandarte* to Wilhelm Mohnke.

What he lacked in personal charisma, Theodor Wisch made up in thorough professionalism, gaining both the respect and affection of the men under his command.

KURT 'PANZER' MEYER

Kurt Meyer of 21st SS Panzer Division became the youngest divisional commander in the German army at the age of 33. The son of a labourer, he was born on 23 December 1910 in Jerxheim. After elementary education, he served first as a miner and then with the forces of the Mecklenburg Land Police.

A firm early supporter of National Socialism (NSDAP No 316714), he joined the SS and received membership no. 17559. His promotion thereafter was fast: *SS-Untersturmführer* in 1932, *SS-Obersturmführer* the next year and *SS-Haupsturmführer* in 1937. Three years previous to the granting of *Haupsturmführer* rank, Meyer had joined the *Leibstandarte*. After serving in Poland and France, he achieved further promotion as *SS-Sturmbannführer* and, as Reconnaissance Detachment commander, went to Greece. This was the scene of his most celebrated achievement, earning him the Knight's Cross on 15 May 1941: storming through the heavily defended Klissura Pass at the head of his unit.

Meyer's role in Kharkov during the Soviet campaign added to his already highly sterling reputation and both the promotion to *SS-Obersturmbannführer* and the addition of Oak Leaves to his Knight's Cross. Further promotion followed in July 1943, when he was transferred to the command of the newly formed 25th SS Panzer Grenadier Regiment of the 12th SS Panzer Grenadier Division *Hitler Jugend* and the granted the rank of *SS-Standartenführer*.

The tough and aggressive fighting force of 'young tigers' who fought under his command in Normandy provided tough opposition to the Allies. Around Caen, there were tough battles against the Canadians.

Right: Michael Wittmann, considered by many to be the foremost tank commander of the war and certainly the most decorated. A star *Leibstandarte* man, he was ultimately advanced to the rank of *SS-Obersturmführer*.

This was by no means the full extent of Meyer's achievements or, indeed, of his promotions. On 1 August 1944, two weeks after assuming control of the 12th SS Division after the death of Fritz Witt, he was, at 33, holding the rank of *SS-Oberführer* and in the same month came the Swords to his Knight's Cross.

On 6 September 1944 he was captured near Amiens. In *Defeat in the West*, published in 1968, Milton Shulman wrote of Meyer: 'He was the perfect product of Nazi fanaticism. Tall, handsome with penetrating blue eyes, he knew only what Hitler had told him, and believed it all. He was prepared to die for his faith in National Socialism and he was utterly ruthless in forcing others to die for it as well … Meyer had neither the training nor the experience to lead 20,000 men and over 200 tanks in battle, but he possessed both a keen tactical sense and the tenacity of a zealot, which enabled him to perform the defensive role required of him at Caen.'

After the war, he was tried as the first German war criminal and found guilty of the murder of 45 Canadian prisoners of war on 8 June 1944. He was sentenced to life imprisonment, but was released 10 years later. He became an active member of HIAG – the Waffen-SS Old Comrades Association – until his death on 23 December 1961. In 1951, he had published his memoirs under the title *Grenadiere*.

WILHELM MOHNKE

Wilhelm Mohnke, who served as commander of the *Leibstandarte* from 20 August 1944 until 6 February 1945, was born in Lubeck on 15 March 1911, the son of a cabinet-maker. He joined the National Socialist German Workers' Party on 1 September 1931, swiftly seeking membership of the SS, where he was assigned to the Lubeck Troop. He served in the 22nd SS Detachment in Schwerin, in which Kurt Meyer also served. Mohnke was chosen by Sepp Dietrich as one

Left: Kurt 'Panzer' Meyer, seen here during Operation Barbarossa. Meyer served with distinction at Kursk, leading to his promotion and eventual command of the *Hitler Jugend* Divison. He was imprisoned after the war.

Right: *SS-Brigadeführer und General Major* Wilhelm Mohnke, leader of the *Leibstandarte* with the rank of *SS-Oberführer* from 20 August 1944 until 6 February 1945. He became Commandant of the Reich Chancellery.

of the original members of *SS-Stabswache Berlin*, one of the forerunners of the *Leibstandarte*.

NEW COMMAND

At the onset of the war in the West, Mohnke took over command of 11 Battalion, rising to the rank of *SS-Obersturmbannführer* by mid-1943. Previously, he had served in the Balkan campaign, where he had lost a foot in a Yugoslavian air attack. On transfer to 12th Division *Hitler Jugend*, he commanded the SS Panzer Grenadier Regiment No. 26 during the battle for Normandy and received the Knight's Cross in July 1944. After the break-out and escape from Falaise, Mohnke was one of the few to lead organised resistance on the western bank of the Seine. He led this *Kampfgruppe* (combat group) until 31 August, replacing the injured Theodor Wisch as the commander of 1st SS Panzer Division *Leibstandarte Adolf Hitler*. Promotion to *SS-Brigadeführer* came on 30 January 1945, but he was forced to relinquish command when he suffered an injury in an air raid, the result of which was ear damage.

On recovery, Mohnke was appointed the commandant of the defence of the Reich Chancellery in Berlin, where he formed *Kampfgruppe Mohnke*. This combat group was made up of nine battalions which included the remnants of 33rd Waffen Grenadier Division SS *Charlemagne*. Mohnke was captured by the Soviets while leading a group of survivors in a break-out attempt from Hitler's bunker. He was imprisoned in solitary confinement until 1949 and remained in captivity for the next six years.

On release, Mohnke desperately sought obscurity, but it was not to be granted. It was revealed that the German Federal Prosecutor had investigated allegations against him concerning the deaths of US and Canadian soldiers, as well as British ones. When it was discovered that the prosecutor had considered the evidence insufficient for prosecution, there were widespread protests from survivors of the massacre at Wormoudt, together with Canadians and Americans who had served in Malmédy and other areas where atrocities had been committed. On 21 April 1988, in the House of Commons, the British Member of Parliament Jeff Rooker asked the Home Secretary, Douglas Hurd, whether he would 'bring to justice the former Nazi officer, Wilhelm Mohnke of Hamburg' in connection with the massacre in 1940 of over 80 unarmed members of the Royal Warwickshire Regiment. It was subsequently made clear by the Foreign and Commonwealth Office, however, that Mohnke was outside the jurisdiction of the British courts and that there was little prospect of seeking his extradition.

Also in 1988, Leslie Aitken, National Chaplain to the Dunkirk Veterans' Association, published *Massacre on the Road to Dunkirk*, with the words 'Wilhelm Mohnke and the Wormoudt Massacre: The Real Evidence' prominently displayed on the jacket. At the time of writing of this book, Wilhelm Mohnke was still alive and residing in Barsbuttel, near Hamburg.

Otto Kumm

Otto Kumm began his service in the SS with the newly formed SS-VT formation *Der Führer*. A native of Hamburg, he had known little of life outside Himmler's black legions, being barely 22 when he joined the Nazi Party and the SS in the same year. During the Western campaign, *SS-Hauptsturmführer* Kumm was awarded the Iron Cross I and II classes, serving as a battalion commander. After service in Russia, he was elevated to *SS-Obersturmbannführer* and became commander of the regiment *Der Führer*, the same regiment which he had originally joined at its formation.

Kumm was a leader of supreme physical fitness, a considerable advantage in Russia where he led his unit in temperatures that were frequently 50 degrees below Centigrade. On 24 February 1942, he was awarded the Knight's Cross. It was well merited since his regiment consisted of just 35 men – all that had survived bitter defensive battles. On 6 April 1943, he became Chief of Staff of 5th SS Panzer Grenadier Division *Wiking*. With the rank of *SS-Oberführer*, the newly promoted *Waffen-SS* stalwart took command of the 7th SS *Freiwilligen-Gebirgs-Division Prinz Eugen* on 2 August 1944 and, in November, attained the rank of *SS-Brigadeführer und Generalmayor der Waffen-SS*.

He came to the *Leibstandarte* as its final commander, winning his Swords on 4 April 1945, before surrendering to captivity a month later along with the remnants of his division.

Left: Field Marshal von Rundstedt inspecting defences in France in 1944 with Kurt Meyer, Fritz Witt and Sepp Dietrich. Von Rundstedt and Dietrich's main point of contact was a shared taste for cognac.

LINEAGE

The pre-SS formations:
Stabswache (SA Control), 1923
Stosstrupp Adolf Hitler (SA Control), 1923
The formation of the SS:
Stabswache, 1925
Schutzstaffel, 1925
The *Leibstandarte* units:
SS-Stabswache Berlin, 1933
SS-Sonderkommando Berlin, (Also, *SS-Sonderkommando Zossen und
   Jüterbog*), 1933
Adolf Hitler-Standarte, 1933
Leibstandarte Adolf Hitler, 1933
Leibstandarte SS Adolf Hitler, 1934
Infanterie-Regiment Leibstandarte SS Adolf Hitler (mot.), 1938
SS-Division Leibstandarte-SS Adolf Hitler, 1941
SS-Panzer-Grenadier-Division Leibstandarte SS Adolf Hitler, 1942
1.SS-Panzer-Division Leibstandarte SS Adolf Hitler, 1944

Campaigns
Saar/Rhineland Occupation 1935
Austrian Occupation 1938
Czechoslovak Occupation 1939
Poland 1939
Western Campaign 1940
Balkan Campaign 1941
Eastern Front 1941–1942
Western Front 1943
Eastern Front 1943
Italian Campaign 1943
Eastern Front 1943
Western Front 1944
Eastern Front 1945

EMBLEM DESIGN

The *Leibstandarte*'s divisional emblem was introduced in early 1941, based upon the word 'Dietrich' (which literally means in German a skeleton key), i.e. a key which will unlock any door. 'Sepp' Dietrich had been the unit's commander since its formation.

   Oakleaves were added beneath the emblem when Dietrich was awarded the Oakleaves to the Knight's Cross in 1943. There were a number of variants to the original design. A different divisional emblem was used during Operation Citadel (the Kursk Offensive) in 1943.

Until 1942

From 1942

From 1943

DIVISIONAL COMMANDERS

1933 – 7.43   *SS-Oberst-Gruppenführer und Generaloberst der Waffen-SS*,
   Josef (Sepp) Dietrich
7.43 – 20.8.44   *SS-Brigadeführer und Generalmajor der Waffen-SS*,
   Theodor Wisch

20.8.44 – 6.2.45   *SS-Standartenführer* (promoted on 4.11.44 to
   SS-Oberführer), **Wilhelm Mohnke**
6.2.45 – 8.5.45 *SS-Brigadeführer und Generalmajor der Waffen-SS*,
   Otto Kumm

Chief Of Staff (as of 1.3.45) *SS-Obersturmbannführer*
   Dietrich Ziemssen

WAR SERVICE

Date	Corps	Army	Army Group	Area
9.39	XIII	8th Army	South	Poland
5.40	X	18th Army	B	Holland
6.40	XXXXIV	6th Army	B	France
7.40	Reserve	–	C	Lothringen
8.40	XXXXV	1st Army	C	Lothringen
9.40 – 10.40	XXV	1st Army	C	Lothringen
11.40	XXV	1st Army	D	Lothringen
12.40 – 2.41	LX	1st Army	D	Lothringen
3.41	XIV	12th Army	–	Bulgaria
4.41 – 5.41	XXXX	12th Army	–	Greece
6.41	refitting	BdE	–	Protectorate
7.41	Reserve	1st Panzer Group	South	Zhitomir
8.41	XXXXVIII	1st Panzer Group	South	Uman
9.41	Reserve	11th Army	South	Cherson
10.41	XXX	11th Army	South	Perekop
11.41 – 12.41	III	1st Pz. Army	South	Rostov, Mius
1.42	III	1st Pz. Army	South	Mius
2.42 – 5.42	XIV	1st Pz. Army	South	Mius
6.42	Reserve	1st Pz. Army	South	Mius
7.42	III	1st Pz. Army	South	Rostov
8.42 – 10.42	SS Panzer Corps	15th Army	D	Normandy
11.42 – 1.43	Reserve (refitting)	–	D	Normandy
2.43	Reserve	OKH	B	Kharkov
3.43	SS Panzer Corps	4th Pz. Army	South	Kharkov
4.43	Reserve	Army Detachment Kempf	South	Kharkov
5.43 – 6.43	refitting	–	South	Kharkov
7.43	II SS	4th Pz. Army	South	Belgorod
8.43	Reserve	–	B	Upper Italy
9.43 – 11.43	II SS	–	B	Upper Italy
12.43	XXXXVIII	4th Pz. Army	South	Zhitomir
1.44	XXXXVIII	4th Pz. Army	South	Vinnitsa
2.44	Reserve	1st Pz. Army	South	Cherkassy
3.44	Reserve	8th Army	A	Cherkassy
4.44	XXIV	1st Pz. Army	North Ukraine	Tarnopol
5.44	Reserve	OKW	–	Belgium
6.44	refitting	15th Army	B	Belgium
7.44	I SS	Panzer Group West	B	Normandy
8.44	LXXX	1st Army	B	Lothringen
9.44	I SS	7th Army	B	Eifel
10.44	LXVI	7th Army	B	Eifel
11.44	refitting	BdE	–	Westphalen (Siegburg)
12.44	Reserve	6th Pz. Army	OB West	Eifel
1.45	XXXIX	5th Pz. Army	B	Ardennes
2.45	Feldherrnhalle (IV)	8th Army	South	Hungary
3.45	Reserve	–	South	Hungary
4.45	I SS	6th Pz. Army	South	Austria
5.45	I SS	6th Pz. Army	Ostmark	Austria

ORDER OF BATTLE

September 1939-March 1944

```
┌─────────────────────┐
│       Regt HQ       │
└─────────────────────┘

┌─────────────────────┐   ┌──────────────────────────────┐
│  I Infantry Battalion│   │ Panzer Reconnaissance Platoon│
│     4 companies     │   └──────────────────────────────┘
└─────────────────────┘   ┌──────────────────────────────┐
┌─────────────────────┐   │      Motorcycle Company      │
│ II Infantry Battalion│   └──────────────────────────────┘
│     4 companies     │
└─────────────────────┘
┌─────────────────────┐
│III Infantry Battalion│
│     4 companies     │
└─────────────────────┘
┌─────────────────────┐
│ Infantry Gun Company │
└─────────────────────┘
┌─────────────────────┐
│  Anti-Tank Company   │
└─────────────────────┘
┌─────────────────────┐
│   Pioneer Platoon    │
└─────────────────────┘
┌─────────────────────┐
│    Supply Troops     │
└─────────────────────┘
```

```
┌─────────────────────┐
│       Div. HQ       │
└─────────────────────┘

┌──────────────────────────┐  ┌──────────────────────────┐
│ SS Panzer Grenadier Regt 1│  │SS Panzer Recce Detachment 1│
│ 3 Battalions (15 companies)│ │       6 companies        │
│    + 5 misc. companies   │  └──────────────────────────┘
└──────────────────────────┘  ┌──────────────────────────┐
┌──────────────────────────┐  │    SS Panzer Regt 1      │
│ SS Panzer Grenadier Regt 2│  │ 2 battalions (8 companies)│
│ 3 Battalions (14 companies)│ │      +2 companies        │
│    + 5 misc. companies   │  └──────────────────────────┘
└──────────────────────────┘
┌──────────────────────────┐  ┌──────────────────────────┐
│SS Panzer Artillery Regt 1│  │ SS Assault Gun Detachment 1│
│  4 battalions (12 batteries)│ │      3 companies         │
└──────────────────────────┘  └──────────────────────────┘
┌──────────────────────────┐  ┌──────────────────────────┐
│ SS Anti-Tank Detachment 1│  │SS Anti-Aircraft Detachment 1│
│      3 companies         │  │   5 companies + 1 platoon │
└──────────────────────────┘  └──────────────────────────┘
┌──────────────────────────┐  ┌──────────────────────────┐
│SS Panzer-Pioneer Battalion 1│ │SS Panzer Signals Detachment 1│
│      4 companies         │  │      2 companies         │
└──────────────────────────┘  └──────────────────────────┘

┌──────────────────────────┐
│      Supply Troops       │
└──────────────────────────┘
```

In mid-1934, the *Leibstandarte*'s duties were extended and, like the other armed SS units, it was enlarged and organised along military lines. In October 1934 it was decided that the unit would be motorised, and as a result by November the *Leibstandarte*'s composition was as shown below:

Staff, with signals platoon and band

I Battalion	13 Company (Motorcycle)
II Battalion	14 Company (Mortar)
III Battalion	One armoured car platoon

The *Leibstandarte* was now officially designated a motorised regiment and by the end of May 1935 its strength had grown to 2660 men (the total strength of the armed SS at the time was 8459 men).

Dietrich's unit continued to expand over the next four years. A fourth battalion was established to provide guard details for the Reich Chancellery in Berlin and the Berghof in Berchtesgaden.

By the time of the invasion of Poland in 1939, the *Leibstandarte* could muster a combat strength of 3700 men, organised into four infantry battalions and supporting units comprising a motorcycle company, a mortar company, an infantry gun company, an anti-tank company, and an engineer platoon. By May 1940 it had gained one more infantry gun company, a light infantry column and an artillery battalion of three batteries of 105mm (4.1in) field guns. Hitler, against the wishes of the army, allowed the further expansion of the *Leibstandarte* to brigade strength after the successful French campaign, and an artillery regiment, an engineer battalion, a signals company and a reconnaissance detachment were raised. By early 1941 the unit consisted of the following:

Headquarters staff

Three battalions, each of three rifle, one machine gun and one heavy company (the latter consisting of two anti-tank gun platoons (37mm (1.47in) and 50mm (1.9in) PAK) and one each of mortars (81mm (3.2in)) and pioneers).

A fourth (heavy) battalion of one light infantry gun company (75mm (2.95in)), one heavy infantry gun company (150mm (5.9in)), one anti-tank gun company (47mm (1.85in) self-propelled), one field gun company (75mm self-propelled) and one anti-aircraft gun company (37mm).

A fifth (guard) battalion of four companies (at Berlin-Lichterfelde).

A reconnaissance detachment with two motorcycle companies, one armoured car company and one heavy company.

An artillery regiment, with one battalion of three batteries (105mm (4.1in)), one mixed battalion of three batteries (two of 150mm and one of 88mm (3.45in) guns) and one light artillery column.

An engineer battalion with three companies, a bridging column and a light engineer column.

A signals detachment with one telephone and one wireless company.

Miscellaneous supply and service units.

For Operation Barbarossa in June 1941 another infantry battalion, an anti-aircraft detachment of three batteries (two of 3.7cm and one of 2cm Flak), a survey battery, a light signals column, and a field hospital were added to *Leibstandarte*'s strength, raising its complement to 10,796 men.

Over a year later, on 9 September 1942, it was announced by the Führer that his Guard should henceforth be known as the *SS Panzergrenadier Division Leibstandarte Adolf Hitler*. Two panzergrenadier regiments had been created from the existing infantry battalions in mid-1942, and an assault gun detachment (*Sturmgeschütz* III) and a self-propelled anti-tank gun detachment (75mm-equipped Marder) had been added to Dietrich's command.

The strength of a typical *Waffen-SS* panzergrenadier regiment in late 1942 was:

Headquarters and band
Escort company: motorcycle despatch platoon and signals platoon.
Three battalions, each of three companies (of three platoons), one machine gun company, and one heavy company, consisting of one (50mm) anti-tank, one light infantry gun and one engineer platoon.
One anti-tank company (self-propelled) (75mm).
One heavy infantry gun company (self-propelled) (150mm).
One anti-aircraft company (self-propelled) (20mm (.79in)).

In January 1942, however, an *Abteilung* (tank battalion) of three companies equipped with PzKpfw IIIs and IVs was added to the unit in a prelude of what was to come. In November the remnants formed part of the two battalions of SS Panzer Regiment 1. The following month two further companies with the new PzKpfw VI Tigers (22 examples in all) arrived. Finally, in the first half of 1943, 100 PzKpfw V Panthers were added to the *Leibstandarte*'s tank arm, which, with a supposed strength of some 250 tanks, was organised as follows:

Headquarters
Three battalions each of four companies, a heavy company and an engineer company.
(However, the third battalion was given up when the division was moved to Italy following the Allied invasion in the autumn of 1943.)

On 22 October 1943 the unit received its final title – *1 SS Panzer Division Leibstandarte Adolf Hitler.*

By the end of 1943 the *Leibstandarte* could muster 19,867 men, little worse than the 20,844 that had been on its books a year previously, and considerably higher than a *Wehrmacht* division.

In March 1944 the *Leibstandarte* could field the following:

Divisional headquarters

SS Panzer-Grenadier Regiment 1
Headquarters
I Battalion with Nos.1–5 Companies
II Battalion with Nos.6–10 Companies
III Battalion with Nos.11–15 Companies
No.16 Anti-aircraft Company
No.17 Infantry gun Company
No.18 Anti-tank Company
No.19 Reconnaissance Company
No.20 Engineer Company

SS Panzer-Grenadier Regiment 2
Headquarters
I Battalion with Nos.1–5 Companies
II Battalion with Nos.6–10 Companies
III Battalion with Nos.11–14 Companies
No.15 Anti-aircraft Company
No.16 Infantry gun Company
No.17 Anti-tank Company
No.18 Reconnaissance Company
No.19 Engineer Company

SS Panzer Reconnaissance Detachment 1
Headquarters
Nos.1–6 Companies

SS Panzer Regiment 1
Headquarters
I Battalion with Nos.1–4 Companies
II Battalion with Nos.5–8 Companies
Heavy Company
Engineer Company

SS Assault Gun Detachment 1
Headquarters
Nos.1–3 Companies

SS Panzer Anti-Tank Detachment 1
Headquarters
Nos.1–3 Companies

SS Anti-Aircraft Detachment 1
Headquarters
Nos.1–5 Companies
20mm (1.45in) Flak Platoon

SS Panzer Artillery Regiment 1
Headquarters
I Battalion with Nos.1–3 Batteries
II Battalion with Nos.4–6 Batteries
III Battalion with Nos.7–9 Batteries
IV Battalion with Nos.10–12 Batteries

SS Panzer Pioneer Battalion 1
Headquarters
Nos.1–4 Companies

SS Panzer Signals Detachment 1
Headquarters
Nos.1–2 Companies

Moved to Belgium in anticipation of an Allied invasion, on 1 June 1944 the *Leibstandarte* comprised 21,386 men, armed with 50 PzKpfw IV, 38 Panther, and 29 Tiger tanks and 45 self-propelled guns. In September a mortar detachment was added:

SS Mortar Detachment 1
Headquarters
Nos.1–3 Batteries (150mm (5.9in))
No.4 Battery

On 20 September the *Leibstandarte*'s strength was supposedly 20,107 (655 officers, 4177 NCOs, 14,246 men and 1,029 helpers).

For Hitler's last great effort, the Ardennes Offensive, the remnants of the *Leibstandarte* formed the infamous *Kampfgruppe Peiper,* which comprised:

I Battalion Panzer Regiment
III Battalion Panzer Grenadier Regiment 2
II Battalion Artillery Regiment
3 Company Pioneer Battalion
Reconnaissance Detachment
68 Flak Battalion (Luftwaffe)

501 Heavy Panzer Battalion (I SS Panzer Corps) (PzKpfw VI Tiger IIs)

The I Panzer Battalion was a mix of the strongest companies:
Headquarters
1 Company (PzKpfw V)
2 Company (PzKpfw V)   60 tanks in total

6 Company (PzKpfw VI)
7 Company (PzKpfw VI)   60 tanks in total

9 Company (Engineers)
Artillery

By this late stage of the war reinforcements were practically nil. On 7 April 1945, a month from the war's end in Europe, the once-proud *Leibstandarte* fighting in Austria could field only 57 officers, 229 NCOs, 1,296 men and 16 tanks.

WAFFEN-SS DIVISIONS 1939–45

Title (and nominal divisional strength at the beginning of 1945)	Granted Divisional Status	Knight's Crosses Awarded
1st SS-Panzer Division *Leibstandarte-SS Adolf Hitler* (22,000)	1942	58
2nd SS-Panzer Division *Das Reich* (18,000)	1939	69
3rd SS-Panzer Division *Totenkopf* (15,400)	1939	47
4th SS-Panzergrenadier Division *Polizei* (9,000)	1939	25
5th SS-Panzer Division *Wiking* (14,800)	1940	55
6th SS-Gebirgs Division *Nord* (15,000)	1941	4
7th SS-Freiwilligen Gebirgs Division *Prinz Eugen* (20,000)	1942	6
8th SS-Kavallerie Division *Florian Geyer* (13,000)	1942	22
9th SS-Panzer Division *Hohenstaufen* (19,000)	1943	12
10th SS-Panzer Division *Frundsberg* (15,500)	1943	13
11th SS-Freiwilligen Panzergrenadier Division *Nordland* (9,000)	1943	25
12th SS-Panzer Division *Hitlerjugend* (19,500)	1943	14
13th Waffen Gebirgs Division der SS *Handschar* (12,700)	1943	4
14th Waffen Grenadier Division der SS (22,000)	1943	1
15th Waffen Grenadier Division der SS (16,800)	1943	3
16th SS-Panzergrenadier Division *Reichsführer-SS* (14,000)	1943	1
17th SS-Panzergrenadier Division *Götz von Berlichingen* (3500)	1943	4
18th SS-Freiwilligen Panzergrenadier Division *Horst Wessel* (11,000)	1944	2
19th Waffen Grenadier Division der SS (9000)	1944	12
20th Waffen Grenadier Division der SS (15,500)	1944	5
21st Waffen Gebirgs Division der SS *Skanderbeg* (5000)	1944	0
22nd SS-Freiwilligen Kavallerie Division *Maria Theresa* (8000)	1944	6
23rd Waffen Gebirgs Division der SS *Kama* (disbanded late 1944, number '23' given to next division)	1944	0
23rd SS-Freiwilligen Panzergrenadier Division *Nederland* (6000)	1945	19
24th Waffen Gebirgskarstjäger Division der SS (3000)	1944	0
25th Waffen Grenadier Division der SS *Hunyadi* (15,000)	1944	0
26th Waffen Grenadier Division der SS (13,000)	1945	0
27th SS-Freiwilligen Grenadier Division *Langemarck* (7000)	1944	1
28th SS-Freiwilligen Grenadier Division *Wallonien* (4000)	1944	3
29th Waffen Grenadier Division der SS (disbanded late 1944, number '29' given to next division)	1944	0
29th Waffen Grenadier Division der SS (15,000)	1945	0
30th Waffen Grenadier Division der SS (4500)	1945	0
31st SS-Freiwilligen Grenadier Division *Böhmen-Mähren* (11,000)	1945	0
32nd SS-Freiwilligen Grenadier Division *30 Januar* (2000)	1945	0
33rd Waffen *Kavallerie* Division der SS (destroyed soon after formation, number '33' given to next division)	1945	0
33rd Waffen Grenadier Division der SS *Charlemagne* (7000)	1945	2
34th SS-Freiwilligen Grenadier Division *Landstorm Nederland* (7000)	1945	3
35th SS-Polizei Grenadier Division (5000)	1945	0
36th Waffen Grenadier Division der SS (6000)	1945	1
37th SS-Freiwilligen Kavallerie Division *Lützow* (1000)	1945	0
38th SS-Grenadier Division *Nibelungen* (1000)	1945	0

WAFFEN-SS RANKS AND THEIR ENGLISH EQUIVALENTS

SS-Schütze	Private	**SS-Hauptsturmführer**	Captain
SS-Oberschütze	Senior Private, attained after six months' service	**SS-Sturmbannführer**	Major
		SS-Oberbannsturmführer	Lieutenant-Colonel
SS-Sturmmann	Lance-Corporal	**SS-Standartenführer**	Colonel
SS-Rottenführer	Corporal	**SS-Oberführer**	Senior Colonel
SS-Unterscharführer	Senior Corporal /Lance-Sergeant	**SS-Brigadeführer und Generalmajor der Waffen-SS**	Major-General
SS-Scharführer	Sergeant	**SS-Gruppenführer und Generalleutnant der Waffen-SS**	Lieutenant-General
SS-Oberscharführer	Staff Sergeant		
SS-Hauptscharführer	Warrant Officer	**SS-Obergruppenführer und General der Waffen-SS**	General
SS-Sturmscharführer	Senior Warrant Officer after 15 years' service	**SS-Oberstgruppenführer und Generaloberst der Waffen-SS**	Colonel-General
SS-Untersturmführer	Second Lieutenant		
SS-Obersturmführer	First Lieutenant	**Reichsführer-SS**	(no English equivalent)

BIBLIOGRAPHY

Ailsby, Christopher, *SS: Roll of Infamy*, Motorbooks International, 1997.

Aitken, Leslie MBE, *Massacre on the Road to Dunkirk: Wormhout 1940*, Patrick Stephens, 1988.

Barker, A. J., *Waffen SS At War*, Ian Allan Publishing, 1982.

Bender, Roger James and Taylor, Hugh Page, *Uniforms, Organization and History of the Waffen-SS* (out of print).

Carrell, Paul, *Scorched Earth: The Russian-German War, 1943-1944*, Schiffer Military History, Atglen, PA, 1994.

Cook, Stan, *Liebstandarte SS Adolf Hitler Volume One: Uniforms, Organisation and History*, R. James Bender Publishing, California, 1994.

Cross, Robin, *Fallen Eagle: The Last Days of the Third Reich*, Michael O'Mara Books Ltd, 1995.

Cross, Robin, *Citadel: The Battle of Kursk*, Michael O'Mara Books Ltd, 1993.

Erickson, John, *The Road to Berlin: Stalin's War With Germany*, Weidenfeld & Nicholson, 1983.

Guderian, Heinz, *Panzer Leader*, Michael Joseph Ltd, 1952.

Hoffmann, Peter, *Hitler's Personal Security*, Macmillan Press Ltd, 1979.

Keegan, John, *Waffen-SS: The Asphalt Soldiers*, Macdonald & Company, 1970.

Kessler, Leo, *The Life and Death of SS Colonel Jochen Peiper*, Leo Cooper/Secker & Warburg, 1986.

Lucas, James, *War on the Eastern Front*, Jane's Publishing Company, 1980.

Lucas, James and Cooper, Matthew, *Hitler's Elite: Leibstandarte SS*, Macdonald & Janes, 1975.

MacDonald, Charles, *The Battle of the Bulge*, Weidenfeld & Nicholson, 1984.

Mann, Chris, *SS-Totenkopf: The History of the 'Death's Head' Division 1940–45*, Spellmount, 2000.

Messenger, Charles, *Hitler's Gladiator: The Life and Times of Oberstgruppenfuhrer und Panzergeneral-Oberst der Waffen SS Sepp Dietrich*, Brassey's, 1988.

O'Donnell, James P., *The Berlin Bunker*, J M Dent & Sons Ltd.

Padfield, Peter, *Himmler Reichsfuhrer SS*, Macmillan, 1990.

Quarrie, Bruce, *Hitler's Samurai: The Waffen-SS in Action*, Patrick Stephens, 1983.

Reitlinger, Gerald, *The SS Alibi of a Nation*, William Heinemann, 1956.

Reynolds, Michael, *The Devil's Adjutant: Jochen Peiper, Panzer Leader*, Spellmount, 1997.

Shirer, William J, *The Rise and Fall of the Third Reich*, Secker and Warburg Ltd, 1959.

Shulman, Milton, *Defeat in the West*, Coronet Books, 1973.

Stein, George H, *The Waffen SS: Hitler's Elite Guard At War*, Oxford University Press, 1966.

Toland, John, *The Last 100 Days*, Arthur Barker, 1965.

Warlimont, Walter, *Inside Hitler's Headquarters 1939-45*, Weidenfeld and Nicholson, 1964.

Weingartner, James J, *Hitler's Guard: The story of SS Leibstandarte Adolf Hitler*, Southern Illinois University Press, 1968.

Whiting, Charles, *Massacre at Malmedy: The story of Jochen Peiper's Battle Group in the Ardennes*, Leo Cooper Ltd, 1971.

Wilmot, Chester, *The Struggle for Europe*, William Collins, 1952.

Windrow, Michael, *Waffen-SS*, Osprey Publishing Ltd, 1992.

The World At Arms: The Reader's Digest Illustrated History of World War II, Reader's Digest Association Ltd, 1989.

Wykes, Alan, *SS Leibstandarte*, Ballantyne Books, 1974.

INDEX